Prospects for Scotland

Report of the
1984 Census of the Churches

Peter Brierley
Fergus Macdonald

A ministry of World Vision
MARC
EUROPE

The National
BIBLE SOCIETY
of Scotland

ISBN (MARC Europe) 0 947697 09 8
ISBN (NBSS) 0 901518 04 2

First printed April 1985

British Library Cataloguing in Publication

Prospects for Scotland: from a census of the churches in 1984.
   1. Church attendance—Scotland—History—Statistics
I. Brierley, Peter   II. National Bible Society of Scotland
306'.6   BR786.3

ISBN 0-947697-09-8

The National Bible Society of Scotland serves the Churches in Scotland by translating and publishing the Word of God and by promoting its distribution and use throughout the country. As a founder member of the United Bible Societies it plays an active role in meeting the growing world-wide demand for the Scriptures. It is located at 7 Hampton Terrace, Edinburgh EH12 5XU.

MARC Europe is an integral part of World Vision, an international Christian humanitarian organisation. MARC's object is to assist Christian leaders with factual information, surveys, management skills, strategic planning and other tools for evangelism. We also publish and distribute related books on mission, church growth, management, spiritual maturity and other topics.

The views expressed by the essayists are not necessarily those held by MARC Europe or The National Bible Society of Scotland.

Contents

ACKNOWLEDGEMENTS

One person in particular has undertaken immense amounts of work for this census – Susan Harrison, now Services Administrator for MARC, but at the time the sorting out of church addresses began, working temporarily with NBSS. She has provided immaculate records, minutely detailed information, and with a thoroughness second to none. Few researchers have the advantage of such a superb organiser, and I would wish to thank her publicly and most warmly for all her efforts.

Likewise many grateful thanks for all the support, concern and detailed work undertaken by Fergus Macdonald, whose enthusiasm for the project has been a continual inspiration, and whose constant help and thoughtful ideas have added greatly to this Report. Apart from these two there have been many others who have helped with telephoning, computerising, mailing, or with numerous other clerical jobs; special thanks are due to Ian Robertson who co-ordinated much of this work. Without such solid support the study would not have been completed so soon, or seen such a high response, and to all these many grateful thanks.

Peter Brierley
April 1985

FOREWORD

Sir DAVID McNEE
President, National Bible
Society of Scotland

Society, largely because of the sophisticated technology available, is better informed and far more enquiring than it has ever been. One aspect of this is that people, particularly the young, no longer appear to take the church seriously, but question her relevance in the kind of world in which we live, and indeed question the need for a faith at all.

I have been reflecting on this and on my own youth while studying the results of the Census. When I was a young man I was closely involved with the Rev. Tom Allan in his work with the "Tell Scotland" Movement, and also in evangelism in this country and Canada.

In the midst of this activity – in the Spring of 1955 – Billy Graham came to the Kelvin Hall, Glasgow, for the "All-Scotland Crusade".

These were miraculous days when the Church and evangelism were given a new impetus and when it was so easy to speak to people about the claims of Christ on their lives. Tom Allan and Billy Graham made evangelism a talking point and the Gospel pertinent to a person's everyday affairs.

Since those challenging times, the churches in Scotland, in my opinion as a mere layman, have lost much of their evangelistic fervour and influence in society. This is particularly concerning now when the need for action is so obvious.

Has there ever been a time when so much is being said about the decline in moral standards and the increase in crime – a lot of it, indeed too much of it, of a serious nature and committed by young people? There is not a day that passes but the media highlight crimes of murder, violence, dishonesty and drug abuse. The problem of evil is around us waiting to be tackled.

That is why I was delighted to learn from the Rev. Fergus Macdonald, General Secretary of the National Bible Society of Scotland, that the Society, together with MARC Europe, was to undertake a Census of church attendance in Scotland. This is the first survey of its kind involving all the denominations and it provides us with information to which we have not hitherto had access.

Someone has said "We won't know where we want to go until we know where we are." As a result of this Report we are now in no doubt where we stand.

This comprehensive Report outlines the needs and opportunities of Christ's mission in Scotland today. It will provide the churches with a most useful tool as they plan to reach the four million Scots who are not regular church attenders.

I commend the Report and would urge all involved and concerned in the Scottish Churches to use it as an instrument which will help them fulfill the task God has called them to do.

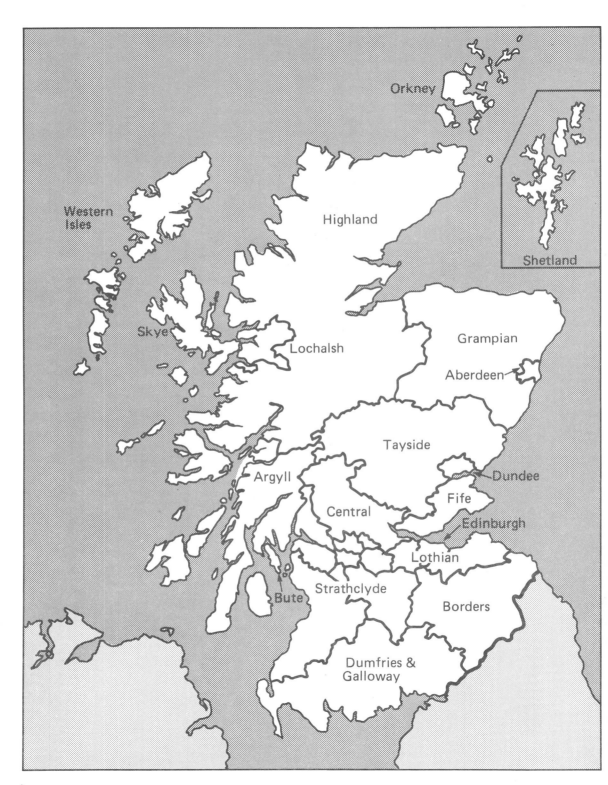

Orkney

Shetland

Western
Isles

Highland

Skye

Lochalsh

Grampian

Aberdeen

Tayside

Argyll

Dundee

Fife

Central

Edinburgh

Lothian

Bute

Strathclyde

Borders

Dumfries &
Galloway

4

INTRODUCTION

Rev FERGUS MACDONALD
General Secretary, National Bible Society of Scotland

This Census could prove, under God, to be a significant catalyst in the renewal and mission of the Scottish Churches as they enter the last decade and a half of the Twentieth Century. The excellent overall response rate of 75 percent indicates that as a whole the Churches recognised the importance of the exercise and hopefully suggests that there will be a willingness now that the results are published to study them and act upon them.

To be fair, some ministers and others were less than enthusiastic about the Census. No doubt there always will be those who feel that statistics are either unspiritual ("Was not David judged for numbering the people"?) or inappropriate ("It's quality, not quantity, that counts"). However, the very positive response from the Churches seems to indicate that reticence was the exception rather than the rule.

Main results

The main results of the Census are as follows:

17 percent of the adult population of Scotland attend church every week. This compares favourably with England (9 percent) and Wales (13 percent).

There are more churches whose attendance is growing than churches whose attendance is declining.

45 percent of all Protestant churchgoers belong to churches which have grown significantly over the four year period 1980 – 1984.

19 percent of all children under 15 attend church regularly which is higher than in England (15 percent), but lower than in Wales (21 percent).

There were more children in church in 1984 than there were in 1980 in relation to the proportion of children in the civil population.

More people belong to the Church of Scotland than any other denomination, but the Roman Catholic Church has most adult attenders and its attendance is declining faster than that of the Church of Scotland.

59 percent of Scottish churches hold mid-week meetings to study the Bible, but these are attended by only 3 percent of the total adult membership.

While Protestant attendance overall declined 2 percent over the period of the survey, this is slower than the decline in church membership (5 percent) and indicates that the fall in church attendance is slowing down.

The Authorised Version is still the most used version of the Bible for Sunday worship and mid-week Bible studies. The Good News Bible (published 1976) has become the next most used version, particularly in mid-week Bible studies.

Qualifications

In the light of the wide support the Census has received it is particularly necessary to bear in mind two important qualifications as we consider the results. The first is the limited nature of the exercise. Church attendance is not the only, nor the most important, criterion of the state of the Church's life, and we must avoid the temptation to evaluate the Census results in isolation from other factors such as the attitudes of Church attenders, their influence in the wider community, etc.

The second qualification is that the whole exercise will turn out to be abortive if the Churches, having supplied the information, feel their involvement is over. In fact it has only begun! Follow-up is even more important than the Census itself. The first Census we read of in the Bible – which, incidentally, gave the Book of Numbers its name – was, as far as we can see, well administered. But then the people of Israel refused to go forward in to the Promised Land and thus failed to fulfil the objective which the census was designed to facilitate. This failure to act in the light of the information the census provided – which the writer to the Hebrews, commenting on the incident, bluntly calls 'unbelief' – led to a wasted forty years in the history of God's people. If, as Paul reminds us, the events recorded in the Book of Numbers 'were written down as a warning for us' (1 Corinthians 10:11), then our Scottish Census, no less than the Israelites', calls for serious reflection and then action in faith. If, as A T Pierson says, 'Facts are the finger of God' there's a message in these statistics for those who have eyes to see.

As we evaluate the Church's mission and plan for the future it is vitally important that we have an accurate picture of what is happening. All too often we are satisfied with hunches and impressions which often turn out to be little more than wishful thinking.

Accuracy

The strength of the Census is that the 1984 figures – which are the results of actual counts taken in congregations – give us the most accurate picture yet available of Church attendance at a given time across the country and the denominations. They provide us not only with local and national attendances – geographically and denominationally – but also with the sex/age profile of normal Sunday congregations, all of which will be of great help to churches and groups of churches as they take stock and lay plans for the future.

The comparisons between 1984 and 1980 require to be interpreted cautiously since it is likely that only in cases where an annual census is regularly undertaken (as in the Roman Catholic Church, the Scottish Episcopal Church and the Methodist Church) does the 1980 attendance entry on the Census forms enjoy the same degree of accuracy as the 1984 figures. Given the human propensity to think there were more people in church last Sunday (or four years ago) than a count would have revealed, estimates tend almost invariably to be high. And this is likely to be the case where the 1980 figure is the result of an estimate rather than a count. This will mean that the decline in some parts of the country and in certain denominations is probably less steep than the figures revealed by the Census indicate. It will also mean that where growth has been recorded this may have been greater than the Census suggests.

Similarly it has to be borne in mind that in relatively sparsely populated rural areas and in the smaller denominations, small differences in attendance figures can produce disproportionately large swings. For example, the growth recorded in the Borders and the decline in the Western Isles, Skye and Lochalsh will require to be interpreted with this in mind.

On the other hand, the Census figures for 1984 and the results of John Highet's research in 1959 give us two firm statistical bases on which to make meaningful general comparisons over a much longer period of time. Over this longer period, the picture is rather discouraging, with the proportion of the adult attendance to the adult civil population having been halved from 26 percent to 13 percent. Protestant attendances have fallen between two and three times faster than Roman Catholic attendance – surely a fact which, when taken alongside other evidence that Protestants in Great Britain are less likely than Catholics to feel the Church meets their various needs (European Values Study, 1982), raises serious questions for Protestants about what they have on offer.

On the other hand, the higher proportion of committed young people in 1984 is a sign of hope, and the discovery of ways and means of harnessing this talent must be a priority in the years ahead. Indeed, the fact that Scotland has today a higher proportion of adults regularly attending church (1 in 6) than have Wales (1 in 8) and England (1 in 11) is a reminder that, despite the decline of the past 25 years, we still have a relatively strong base for mission and service provided the laity can be motivated and trained.

Encouragement and warning

The Census contains both encouragements and warnings for churches in all parts of the country and in all the denominational groups. For example, the Baptists can rightly rejoice in the 4 percent increase in their membership and attribute this to their strong emphasis on evangelism. But indications of falling attendance may be a danger signal that members' commitment is beginning to flag. Taking another example, the Conservative Presbyterians must be concerned that they have a lower percentage of children and a higher percentage of over sixty-fives in relation to their membership than any other denominational group. But they can take courage from their strong leadership potential – they have the highest proportion of men among attenders, and in the 45 – 64 age group they are in a relatively healthy position.

Rightly interpreted the Census will produce neither triumphalism nor despair; in fact it will help churches to build on their strengths in order to consolidate where they are weak.

What now?

We have already said that to count and not to act will make the whole exercise futile and faithless. There is, of course, no way in which this Report can prescribe how each church should use the Census results. Each local church, circuit, presbytery, deanery, diocese, synod and denomination will have to make up its own mind on this. But we offer the following broad suggestions in the hope that they might help to stimulate study which will lead to action:

1. Every local church might appraise its life and witness in the light of the wider picture the Report gives of attendance in its geographical area and throughout its denomination. Should the local church situation be below average in each case, what lessons are there to be learned from other churches? If it is above average, what help can be offered to other churches?

2. Groups of churches, both within the same denomination – as presbyteries, deaneries, dioceses, etc – and across denominations – as Councils of Churches, local committees, etc., – might make a similar study with a view to answering the question: "What is the Report saying to us about the mission of the Church today?" Where there is growth in a given geographical area, steps might be taken to identify the growing churches, analyse the reasons for their growth, and consider what, if any, lessons the static and declining churches might learn.

3. At both the local and the wider levels some attempt might profitably be made to correlate attendances (movement from the community into the churches) with the social influence of churches (the activity of church members in the wider community).

4. The age profile of the churches within geographical areas and denominations might be taken into account in planning future requirements of ministry and plant. Variations from the profile of the civil population may offer clues about the effectiveness of the churches' impact and suggest areas in which their witness requires to be strengthened. Churches may also wish to consider ways of making and building up contacts with people who are in the middle years of life and have ceased to attend public worship, with a view to providing bridges over which this group can cross back into the church when they get older and become more free of the demands of work and family.

5. The Census results indicate that a significant number of churches (28 percent) seem not yet to have sampled the newer versions of the Bible. The Census results, together with the article on Bible Use on page 26, might be a very helpful context in which such churches could re-assess the usefulness of its version of the Bible for its task. After all, Jesus teaches us in the Parable of the Sower that the seed of the Kingdom is the Word of God which bears fruit in those 'who hear the message and understand it' (Matthew 13:13).

6. Another parable – the Lost Sheep (found in Matthew 18: 10-14 and Luke 15: 1-7) – may also point the way forward and might form an appropriate basis for groups to consider the Report in the context of Bible study. After all, it details action taken after a count of the flock revealed a loss of 1 percent. Further, its double application relates to two vitally important aspects of the Church's mission – nurture (in Matthew) and outreach (in Luke) – which the Report is challenging us to think through afresh. Again, it underlines the importance of a

caring attitude and a practical concern for both those whose faith is weak and those who are outside the Church. And finally, it tells us that God deeply cares for people and that we offend Him greatly if we ignore those who lose their faith or despise those who have none.

Conclusion

A special thank you is due to Peter Brierley of MARC Europe who has borne the burden of the Census preparation, collation and analysis more than any other. His wide experience and very considerable expertise in the field of statistics have played a key role in the project.

Our thanks are also due to the very many people in local churches all over the country who carried out the count and returned the Census form. We owe them a very real debt.

Finally, in response to some who have asked: "What has a Bible Society to do with a Census of church attendance?", let me say four things:

First, the Census has been a joint endeavour, with MARC Europe playing the greater part. MARC Europe is a body which specifically carries out exercises of this kind to help the Churches fulfil their mission.

Second, the Bible Society, as a body enjoying the goodwill of all denominations, was in a unique position to commend the Census to the Scottish Churches.

Third, the Society was convinced that a more accurate picture of church attendance would help to facilitate the mission of the Churches and thus stimulate the use of the Word of God.

Fourth, the Society believed that the Census would provide strategic information to help in planning its future work of promoting the distribution and use of the Scriptures throughout Scotland.

TRENDS IN ATTENDANCE AND MEMBERSHIP

DR JOHN HIGHET
Author of books on
Scottish church
Statistics

For much of their history a remarkable feature of British National Churches has been their apparent lack of interest in finding out in a systematic way what proportion of their following regularly attend the services of public worship made available to them.

I found this, to my surprise, in the late 1940s when I started gathering statistics about the Churches in Scotland. Most – though not all – had official records regarding their membership strength (as variously defined); none had quantitative data, centrally recorded, about their members' attendance performance and very few congregations could supply anything other than subjective impressions regarding how their local personnel measured up in this respect. When I extended my investigations south of the Border I found that a similar situation obtained in England and Wales.

An exception to this generalisation can be claimed on behalf of church people of 135 years or so ago who, as a result of a singular historical happening, knew, or were told about, official figures concerning their church-going practice, for in 1851, for the first and only time, a question about attendance at public worship was included in the United Kingdom Census of Population. When, however, this question was dropped from subsequent Census forms no Church body (at least to my knowledge) took it upon itself to continue the flow of such information on its own account by taking regular or even periodic enumerations of its worshippers. It was not until about 100 years after the official UK religious census that this gap was partially closed. This was by an attendance survey carried out in the early 1950s as part of my continuing research, and it was closed only marginally because that survey chiefly (though not solely) concerned the city of Glasgow. Later, further research produced attendance data for Scotland in 1959, though lack of resources at that time made this investigation less extensive in its scope than I would have liked. No such similar research was being carried out for England or for Wales, so far as I could find out.

It is true that from time to time commercial survey agencies commissioned by various agencies (sometimes, for example, by a newspaper) have carried out polls of "religious adherence" or "religious practices" or the like, and these usually produce figures on church attendance. The sad truth is, however, that these data are generally of limited value and are open to much misinterpretation. This is because they frequently adopt inaccurate terminology and set their results in a conceptually questionable framework, sometimes coming up with quite unsatisfactory – not to say ludicrous – correlations. This is especially true of their findings as they apply them to Scotland. I know of some England-based surveys which have grouped all those church members not professing allegiance to an English or a Welsh denomination within the all-embracing and manifestly fatuous category, "Scottish Church". I know, too, of polls which have expressed, say, the membership of the Church of Scotland as a proportion of the population of the UK, implying if not actually stating that, as the small percentage they have come up with shows, that Church is but a poor "also-ran" in the religious statistics stakes.

The recent Census of the Churches in England (undertaken by the British and Foreign Bible Society for the Nationwide Initiative in Evangelism), that of the Churches in Wales (by the British and Foreign Bible Society and published jointly with MARC Europe) and this present Census of Church Attendance in Scotland, March, 1984 (by the, Bible Society of Scotland in collaboration with MARC Europe) are thus greatly to be welcomed as fulfilling the long-standing need for information necessary for the Churches' action-planning and others of their purposes and, at the same time, as of value to the sociologist of religion.

From both points of view – that of the Churches and that of the sociologist of religion – the 1984 census provides a mass of fascinating information relating not only to that year but to 1980 also. This chapter comments in part on attendance and membership trends apparent over that four-year period. However, a period of four years is a rather short one for really significant movements to manifest themselves. Accordingly, since relevant data exist for 1959, I have also brought out indications of trends over these 25 years. Very seldom is it possible to have this sort of follow-up to research done a quarter of a century earlier, and we are singularly fortunate that the 1984 Census affords us this opportunity.

A Note on the 1959/1984 Comparisons

There is one very important point we must bear in mind about the 1959/1984 comparisons. The 1984 Census defined "adult", when applied to population, attenders and members, as meaning "persons aged 15 and over". By contrast, from the start of my church researches in the late 1940s, I took "adult" as "aged 20 and over". I did this because, although I was aware that there were some church members under the age of 20, I was advised at the time that these formed a small group in relation to total membership. Accordingly, it seemed to me that to lower the age-line to (say) 15 years old would mean that when expressed as a percentage of the population aged 15 and over the numerical strength of the Churches would come out unnecessarily depressed. Perhaps I was wrongly advised about the church situation in this respect almost 40 years ago: certainly, as the 1984 data show, the situation has changed and there is now quite a sizable proportion of

Church members and attenders who are aged 15-19 – this, indeed, is one of the census's most notable findings. At all events, having started my enquiries on the "age basis" described, I naturally retained that in all subsequent research for comparison purposes. My 1959 population, attenders, and members figures are thus of persons aged 20 and over.

This, if somewhat unfortunate from our present point of view, is nonetheless understandable: regrettable though it may be, it often happens that different researchers adopt different definitions and category boundaries. Perhaps even more unfortunate is the fact that there is no universally accepted definition of the concept, "church member": different denominations, requiring different kinds and degrees of avowal, define it differently. Indeed, the Roman Catholic Church does not speak of "membership" at all, but of "the Roman Catholic population", which includes not only children but infants. This posed a problem for the 1984 census as, in the past, it had posed one for me. I dealt with it applying the proportion of the country's population aged under 20 to the Catholic population and subtracing this number from the latter figure. This, admittedly, was but an estimate but the figure which resulted seemed one that could more fairly be compared with non-Roman Catholic Churches' numerical strength than could "Catholic population". The 1984 census, on the other hand, accepted Roman Catholic population figures unmodified.

For these reasons I have had to adjust the 1984 figures, when comparing these with my earlier data, to make their base more in line with that of the latter. To spell out and justify these adjustments in every case would be tedious for the reader and would leave little room in this chapter for anything else. I ask the reader to accept that there are no ulterior motives behind this exercise and that I have carried it out as trustworthily as I know how; and I must stress that the responsibility for these adaptations rests with me and with me alone.

With few exceptions I have (as requested) rounded percentages up and down to the nearest whole number.

Finally, I recognise that paragraph after paragraph packed, as here, with figures and reiterated wording does not make for easy perusal. I ask the reader to be patient. It is not expected that the data here presented will necessarily be absorbed at one go: they are recorded for periodic consultation as need arises or interest prompts.

Trends, 1980/84 and 1959/84

Between 1980 and 1984, despite a 1% increase in the adult population, there was a 3% fall in the membership of all Churches. This was matched by a similar fall in the number of adult attenders. There thus appears to have been neither an improvement nor a sliding back in the percentage of members who actually attend church. This, however, does not apply to individual Churches and groups of Churches. When we look at the results more closely, interesting differences emerge. The Protestant Churches registered a slightly greater membership than attendance decline (5% and 2% respectively) while the Roman Catholics, with but a marginal drop in membership, showed a 3% fall in attendance. Over this four-year period, then, Catholics were attending rather less well, and Protestants slightly better, than might have been expected from the changes in their respective sizes. We can see this also from considering their attendance-to-membership (or, in the

Catholics' case, population) proportions in these two years. For the Catholics, in 1980 this was 36%; in 1984 it was slightly lower, at 35%. For the Protestants, the proportions were 34% in 1980 and 35% in 1984 – the same as the Catholics. Indeed, in 1984 there was a very interesting three-way parity of attendance/membership proportion, for not only was this 35% for Protestants and Catholics, it was also 35% for all Churches.

We shall later review the attendance performances by selected Protestant Churches, but while the above proportions are before us, let us note the following attendance/membership percentage "scores": Baptist, 107 (this clearly including a number of persons, perhaps "visitors", interested but not committed to membership); Independent Churches, 76; Other Denominations, 75; Conservative Presbyterian, 68; Scottish Episcopal, 40; and Church of Scotland, 29. This latter was the only one lower than the RC "score". This is an interesting finding, because it is generally thought that the obligation on Catholics to attend Mass will have more effect than the non-Roman Catholic Churches' expecting of their following duly to attend public worship. However, although somewhat inferior to Protestants as a group in terms of attendance, the Catholics did better than Protestants – and, for example, the Church of Scotland – with regard to numerical strength, just failing by 1,700 to hold on to their population size in 1980. By contrast, Protestant membership fell by 51,360, including a fall in Church of Scotland membership of 46,020.

This is also a suitable place at which to note that the Church of Scotland score in 1984 of 29% (attendance as a percentage of membership) was marginally better than its score for 1980. Expressed, this time, to one decimal place to show the trend, its attenders/members percentages in these years were: 28.5 in 1980 and 29.3 in 1984. Over this 4-year period its membership fell by 5% while the number of its attenders dropped by 2%.

Here we might also note that Roman Catholic churches are few in number but large in attendance; by contrast, Protestant churches are more numerous but have smaller gatherings of worshippers. The Church of Scotland has 44% of all churches in the country as against the Roman Catholics' 15%.

Let us now look at comparisons over the longer period, 1959 to 1984 (remembering that, to be consistent with the 1959 data, "adult" now means "aged 20 and over", and bearing in mind that when constituent percentages do not add up exactly to appropriate totals, this is because of rounding-off). Total adult attenders in 1984 made up 13% of the total adult population. In 1959 they represented 26%. Taking Protestant and Roman Catholic attenders separately, we find that the former represented 7% of the population in 1984 compared with 17% in 1959, and the latter 6% compared with 10%. The level of Catholic attendance is thus lower now than it was 25 years ago – but only to between one-half and one-third of the extent applying to Protestants.

In terms of proportion to all-Churches' adult membership (this latter term including the Roman Catholic population adjusted as required) in 1984 total adult attenders represented 35% compared with 44% in 1959. For adult Protestant attenders the percentages were 20% (1984) and 28% (1959), and for Roman Catholics, 15% and 16%. Here again we see that over this 25-year period Protestants have made by far the greater contribution to the overall attendance fall. This puts in perspective what the shorter-period contrast brought out, *viz.*, the Catholic failure then to maintain their traditional superior attendance practice over that of the Protestant Churches.

However, if Protestants shoulder most of the responsibility for the attendance decline over this quarter-century, the blame for this lies overwhelmingly with the Church of Scotland (as indeed is to be expected from that Church's position as by far the largest Protestant denomination). Church of Scotland adult attenders in 1984 were 5% of the adult population compared with 13% in 1959, and 14% of total adult church membership compared with 21%.

Yet the decline in the Church of Scotland attendance level is not as spectacular as is that shown by the Catholics. As we have already seen, in 1984 the attenders/members "score" for the Catholics was 35% and the comparable score for the Church of Scotland 29%. Twenty-five years earlier the scores were 63% for the Catholics and 34% for the Church of Scotland. The narrowing of this gap and the greater relative decline in Catholic attendance performances are features of the quarter-century as surprising as they are noteworthy.

Other indications of the changes in Catholic, Protestant, and specifically Church of Scotland, attendance practice over this period should be noted. (Here again I am expressing values in fractions of whole numbers in order to show the movement.) In 1959 there were 1.7 adult Protestant attenders for each adult Catholic attender; in 1984 this had become 1.3 : 1. In 1959 there were 1.3 adult Church of Scotland attenders to each adult Catholic attender; by 1984 the ratio was round the other way. Then it was a little under 1.1 Catholic for each Church of Scotland attender.

There have also been notable changes in relative numerical strength. These are discussed in a later section. We pass on now to consider the shorter-period and the longer-period trends relating to other Churches. Over the four years the Baptist Churches showed a 4% fall in the number of attenders despite a 4% rise in membership. This decline in attendance is, however, largely on the part of the "Other Baptists" (the "reformed" Baptists, Grace (Strict) Baptists, and Independent Baptists). As a group, these recorded an 18% drop in attendance against an 8% increase in membership. The Baptist Union of Scotland also showed some fall away in attendance, but not to such an extent. In their case, there was a 1% fall in the numbers attending despite a rise in membership of a little over 3%. However, this should be seen as an uncharacteristic, and possibly temporary, back-sliding. For example, in 1959 Baptist Union attenders represented 78% of membership (excluding adherents); in 1984, attenders were 107% of members-plus-adherents (some interested but not committed visitors also being included in this figure). While an exact comparison is not possible, the Baptist Union level of attendance does seem to have increased quite impressively over that 25-year period. How does this relate to trends in membership? Members (excluding adherents) numbered 20,139 in 1959; in 1984, members and adherents numbered 17,310 – a drop of 2,829 (and of more than that if adherents were deducted from the 1984 figure). Thus, their 1984 higher attendance level was achieved despite a fall in membership. Baptists, good attenders 25 years ago, are even better attenders now. This is a distinction that can be claimed by very few other Churches.

Between 1980 and 1984, the Scottish Episcopal Church and Other Denominations both showed an absolute increase in attenders (of 9% and 1% respectively) although membership had fallen – in each case by 3%. Episcopal Church attenders were 40% of membership in 1984 and 35% in 1980. In 1959, the percentage was 40%. Despite the small back-sliding over the past 4 years, then, members have now re-established their attendance level of 25 years ago. Their number has fallen by 28,391 between 1959 and 1984 and by 1,350 in the four years since 1980.

Poor attendance performances were turned in by the group of Conservative Presbyterian Churches. In their cases, 1984 saw a 10% fall in attenders compared with 1980 against a 9% drop in membership. I found this surprising, because this category includes, for example, the Free Church of Scotland which my late-1950s research had shown to have the relatively good attendance "score" of 54%. I cannot compare this with a score for 1984, since that year's Census does not separate the Free Church data from Reformed Presbyterian returns. However, a justifiable suspicion is that in the Free Church the level of attendance has declined markedly since 1959. It seems very likely, too, that there has been a fall – perhaps not inconsiderable – in this Church's membership. The Free Presbyterian Church registered a 16% decrease in the number of members-plus-adherents from 4,750 in 1959 to 4,165 in 1984. I have no 1959 attendance information for the Free Presbyterians, but their attendance showing between 1980 and 1984 was not at all impressive: it went down by 16% as against a members-plus-adherents fall of 12%.

In the analyses of the 1984 and the 1980 data, a number of relatively small Churches are grouped together in the categories "Independent" and "Other Denominations". I select a few of these for comment. Over these four years, the Methodist Church registered an 8% drop in attenders against a 12% drop in members. The worshippers still in membership were therefore attending rather more regularly; but in 1984, 55% of members attended, compared with 63% in 1959. The membership went down over the same period by 39%.

Like the Methodists, the United Free Church (included in "Other Denominations") showed a better attendance performance, in relation to the fall in membership, in 1984 compared with four years previously. Over that period membership fell by 9% but attendance by 5%. However, in 1984 proportionately more members were turning out compared with their predecessors in 1959, when 43% of members attended, as against 49% in 1984.

The Congregational Union also improved its attendance record between 1980 and 1984, between which dates membership fell by 7% but attenders by 3%. Like the UF Church, but unlike most of the bodies considered in this chapter, it slightly bettered its attendance record in 1984, when 51% of members attended, compared with 49% in 1959. But over these 25 years there has been a considerable fall in adult membership (as defined in this section's discussion) – by 64% from 34,495 in 1959 to 12,292 in 1984.

Area Variations

We now take a quick glance at the attendance and membership movements in selected areas of Scotland between 1980 and 1984.

Those where attendance is dropping fastest are the Western Isles (against a population increase), Lothian (including the City of Edinburgh), and the City of Glasgow. Those showing most growth are Grampian outside Aberdeen (reflecting the population increase there brought about by increasing employment opportunities), the Borders Region, and the Eastwood, Bearsden-plus-Milngavie, and Strathkelvin parts of Strathclyde.

These three last-mentioned districts also show significant increase in membership; these, indeed, are the only places to show this trend. This, and the attendance growth, may well reflect the increase there in Catholic residents. There is some growth in the Highlands, Grampian Region, and the Motherwell and Monklands districts of Strathclyde – again not unconnected with Catholic presence. However, overall membership is declining across virtually the whole of Scotland. It is declining most in Lothian (including Edinburgh) and in the Western Isles.

Church of Scotland attendance is declining fastest in the city areas of Aberdeen, Edinburgh, the centre of Glasgow, in Lothian (apart from Edinburgh) and Renfrew and Inverclyde, and in Shetland, the Western Isles and Skye and Lochalsh. In all these areas, turn-out fell by 6% or over in the four years. Yet in terms of membership, the National Church is strong in the Central Region and in these city areas and in Grampian outside Aberdeen. So in some areas there is decline in attendance where there is still some strength in membership. The Church of Scotland is also quite strong in the Highlands, the Grampian Region outside Aberdeen, and in Fife, where there is also some growth in attendance.

The Conservative Presbyterian Churches are numerically strong in three areas – the Western Isles with Skye and Lochalsh, the Highland area including Argyll and Bute, and the City of Glasgow. But these places have lost on average 10% of their attenders in the last four years. These Churches have suffered a membership fall also, though this is less than the drop in attendance.

Episcopal Church attendance increased through-out Scotland but membership is declining over the whole country.

Baptists are strongest numerically in Edinburgh, Glasgow City, and to the west, south and east of Glasgow (except for Eastwood). So far as their 1980-84 fall in attendance is concerned, there are considerable geographical variations – Fife and Edinburgh, for example, show the steepest rate of decline.

For at least one area we can make a comparison between attendance levels in 1984 and at an earlier date – this time, 30 years previously. My research into the Church situation in the city of Glasgow in the early 1950s, though not including all the city's denominations, covered eight – the Church of Scotland, the Baptist Union, the Congregational Union, the Episcopal Church, the Free Church, the Methodist Church, the United Free Church, and the Roman Catholic Church – and taken together these embraced about 98% of the estimated total church membership in the city. In the spring of 1954, when with these bodies' co-operation I took a Census of Church Attendance, 20% of the city's adult population attended the above Churches' services. This compares with 19% in 1984. The 1954 proportion would, of course, have been a little higher had some Churches not been unavoidably left out. As proportions of the city adult church membership the attendances were 37% in 1954 and between 35% and 36% in 1984. Here again the 1954 percentage would have

been somewhat higher had the census been of all Churches, since some of those omitted are generally thought to have quite high attendance scores. We can then say that, related to both population and membership, the attendance level in Glasgow is lower than it was 30 years ago, but not notably. However, if we take the attendance figures by themselves, we can see that the annual rate of decline is increasing: there was a drop of 44% between 1954 and 1984, or 1.5 per year, compared with a 7% drop between 1980 and 1984, or 1.8 per year. And certainly the Church of Scotland attendance level is falling drastically and at an increasing rate. In 1984, adult attendance in Glasgow (here taken as aged 20 and over) was 22,464 compared with 45,294 in 1954 – a fall of 50% or 1.6% per year. Between 1980 and 1984, the decline was 12%, or 3% per year. Relatively to adult population in the city, Church of Scotland adult attenders were 6% in 1954 and 4% in 1984.

The main membership changes since 1959: further discussion

So far, we have been primarily concerned with trends in attendance between 1980 and 1984 and between 1959 and 1984. In what is part of an analysis of the Scottish Church Attendance Census, 1984, this is entirely as it should be. However, attendance is but one aspect of the Churches' strength in human terms; one of the others is membership. It can be argued that, of the two, membership is of more crucial importance than attendance, in that if a denomination seeks to improve its following's attendance it has, if not quite a "captive audience" to work on, at least a list of the names and addresses of the people who might be contacted to that end. On the other hand, increasing its membership will generally involve going out among the "churchless masses" in an effort to attract some of them to their fellowship. This requires more effort, more time, and much more money, and is for other reasons the more difficult exercise.

Further, membership is the more primary index of the extent of a society's religious affiliation.

Size of and trends in membership, absolute and relative, are, then, a matter of considerable interest not only to the churchman but to the sociologist of religion – and, indeed, to the general sociologist, to whom these indicate important aspects of a society's culture (here using that term in the sociologist's sense). In this section, I propose to deal specifically with trends in the membership of Scotland's main religious groupings, setting these in the broader context of a major and traditional element in the country's culture. The churchman, to whom the main membership changes speak directly, will not, I think, find the comments pertaining to the latter topic in any way irrelevant.

Since the Reformation of 1560 Scotland has been predominantly a Protestant and, within that, a Presbyterian country. This was still true 25 years ago, when 44% of the adult population were Protestant adult church memers, 39% were Presbyterian, and 15% were Roman Catholics (estimated adults). Within the total adult church membership, 74% were Protestant, 66% Presbyterian, and 26% Roman Catholic. The Church of Scotland – the National Church, "established yet free" – was far and away the largest single denomination, having 1,315,466 members, representing 38% of the adult population and 64% of total church membership.

By 1984, the position had changed quite markedly. Then

the proportion of the adult population who were adult members of Protestant Churches had fallen to 27% – the great bulk of them, however, still Presbyterian – and the proportion who were Catholics had risen to 16%. Within the total adult church membership, 63% were Protestants and 37% were Catholics.

Another way of putting this is to say that whereas in 1959 there were very nearly 3 Protestants for every Catholic, the ratio is now 1.7-to-one.

So far as the Church of Scotland is concerned, in this quarter-century the ratio of its adult members to Roman Catholics has changed from nearly 2.5-to-one to 1.7:1. This has come about not so much because of notable growth in the adult Roman Catholic population as because of a marked fall in Church of Scotland membership. This decline continued during the shorter of our two review periods: to remind ourselves, between 1980 and 1984 its membership fell by 5%.

By 1984 the Church of Scotland, while still the largest single denomination, had ceased to be that by anything like the margin applying earlier, though it could still claim the majority of the religiously affiliated citizens of Scotland, with its adult membership out-numbering, by itself, that of all other Churches put together.

However, considering that, along with the long-established Jewish community, there are now within Scotland's borders many thousands of Asian immigrants affiliated to the Moslem or Hindu faiths, and that they, like the Roman Catholic population, probably have a higher birth-rate than the country's Protestants, the realistic expectation is that, unless there is a spectacular growth in Church of Scotland membership, an even more pronounced change in Scotland's religious structure will take place.

For the churchman with a Scottish historical sense, as well as for the sociologist, such a development would call for reflection. Scotland has been, for many centuries, a Presbyterian nation culturally as well as in terms of her predominant religious faith. Much in her traditional values – secular as well as spiritual – stems from her Presbyterian moulding: much more than (for example) what some critics like to describe dyslogistically and not always justifiably as her "suffocating Calvinism". Even if by this change she loses nothing religiously, one might ask oneself: for how long will her culture keep that Presbyterian flavour as this new situation prevails and, perhaps, gathers momentum?

What should be the Churches' Response?

In my book, *The Scottish Churches* (Skeffington, 1960), in which I reported on my late-1950s research findings, I wrote: "For Scotland to have only 59% of its adults in full membership of its Christian Churches may seem a poor showing for a country with a reputation for being 'church-minded'." What should one's verdict be to-day, when the proportion of its adult population who are members of a Church is 37%? (Here again "adult" – to allow 1959/1984 comparisons – is taken as "aged 20 and over".) This would seem to suggest that the reputation is scarcely justified.

However, if "adult" is defined (as mostly in this book) as "aged 15 and over", we find that 43% of the adult population are Church members and a further 4% are Catholic church members under the age of 15. This puts a different complexion on the situation, and may well justify the opinion of Mr Brierley (for example) that "the strength of

Christianity in Scotland remains relatively high". And what this latter figure clearly demonstrates is that the Churches are winning relatively more support from those aged 15-19 than from their seniors. That gives the churchman much encouragement as he looks to the future.

Nonetheless, the story is, on the whole, one of diminishing support of their Churches by the people of Scotland, both over the past 4 years and over the last quarter-century. The Roman Catholics now have a greater share than previously of committed Christians but latterly their growth has been marginal. Among Protestant Churches the vast majority show falling attendance levels and – with one exception, the Baptist Union – declining membership (and even that Church showed a decrease in attendance between 1980 and 1984). Further, if 17% of the entire Scottish adult population attend church, clearly 83% – almost 4,200,000 – do not; and in Mr Brierley's words, this is "an astonishingly large number of people".

What are the causes of this general decline? Ideally, a commentary of this kind should end by listing a set of cogent reasons and suggesting profitable lines of action the Churches might take to counter the causes. I could suggest a few causes, but this would not be at all helpful because these would be largely such as would occur to anyone who ponders the problem. Beyond that, I could not go very far; nor, I think could many of us. It will take much research by the Churches to find the definitive answer to the question just posed.

Meantime, someone might suggest that one way to arrest the decline in membership and attendance is for the Churches to stage a campaign of mass evangelism. In the hope that to do so may be helpful I should like to finish by reporting on my findings regarding the extend of the impact on attendance practice and membership strength of the Billy Graham/Tell Scotland Crusade of 1955.

With the co-operation of seven non-Roman-Catholic denominations I carried out a Church Attendance Census in the city of Glasgow on three Sundays in the spring of 1954. The seven were the Church of Scotland, the Baptist Union, the Congregational Union, the Episcopal Church, the Free Church, the Methodist Church, and the United Free Church. (The Roman Catholic Church also took part on this occasion, but they withdrew from the two follow-up censuses, so I am excluding the Roman Catholic data from this summary.) That 1954 census, it should be noted, was organised as part of the research on which I was then engaged: in initiating it there was no thought of how it would come to serve as part of a measure of Crusade effectiveness. However, in due course the Billy Graham/ Tell Scotland campaign was organised, and the seven Churches and I decided to take another census almost exactly a year later, starting on Sunday 1st May, 1955 – just a few hours after Dr Graham's closing rally on Saturday, 30th April – and continuing on 8th and 15th May. This meant that we had a pre-Graham base-line of attendance with which to compare the level of attendance immediately "after Graham".

The results showed that in 1955 average three-Sunday attendance by members of the seven Churches had risen by 10,575 compared with the three-Sunday average the year before. We then decided to carry out a third census exactly a year later, to see how many of the "new attenders" were still in the pews. The 1956 returns showed a fall in the number of attenders of 4,854. Thus, one year after the Crusade about half of the attenders gained had fallen away.

Further, other enquiries – this time by means of a Scotland-wide sample of ministers – revealed that the vast majority stated that their experience was that the Graham Crusade had had "little effect or none at all" in increasing membership – though (interestingly enough) a slight majority of Baptist ministers said, "Decided effect or slight effect".

As a tribute to the ministers, office-bearers, and others in these seven Churches who took part in this "combined operation", I add that Dr Graham, who knew of its findings, not merely accepted them but described this follow-up survey as the most systematic investigation ever carried out into the *measurable* impact of a campaign of his.

I think, therefore, that it might fairly be asked if effects of these modest dimensions are worth the time, effort and money expended on crusade-type evangelism. Unless subsequent campaigns by Dr Graham, Dr Luis Palau, and others can point to more impressive measurable – and *measured* – effects, the Churches' efforts to arrest decline should, it might be thought, lie in other directions.

GEOGRAPHY AND RELIGION IN SCOTLAND

R D KERNOHAN
Editor, "Life and Work"

"Geography is about maps, but biography is about chaps." One cannot make so clear-cut a distinction between the natural and the human factors in writing about geography and religion in Scotland.

Glasgow and Edinburgh are little more than 40 miles apart, with only a gentle watershed between the Clyde and Forth valleys. But, if one comes from one to speak in the other, there is always a good response to an opening joke about having crossed the great divide.

For such a small country Scotland is rich in great divides – natural, economic, cultural, political, historical and for that matter theological.

The most obvious natural and historic division is of Lowland and Highland; but both these terms are gross over-simplifications. For example, the historic division of Gaelic Scotland from the rest of the country speaking "Inglis" or Scots (and at the Reformation, using the English Bible) no longer coincides with any clear natural features, except in the Western Isles. There is indeed a great divide between the Central Belt which contains more than three-quarters of Scotland's population in a fraction of its area, but the cultures (and not least the religious cultures) of the islands and the periphery can differ as much from each other as from either Glasgow or Edinburgh. Orkney and Shetland are closer to Scandinavia, in mood as well as history, than to the Hebrides. Galloway is arguably, in some ways, more remote from some trends of modern Scottish life than the greater part of the Highlands. But there are several other great divides to which geography contributes and in which attitudes to religion often becomes a factor, especially in the parts of Scotland where the Roman Catholic fifth of the population is concentrated.

There is the division of West and East – most obvious in the rivalry of Glasgow and Edinburgh but epigrammatically expressible as the difference between coasts looking to Ireland and to Scandinavia.

There is the division of the cities and suburbs from the small towns and countryside – though one does not need to be a Marxist to argue that urban class differences within the city areas may be culturally more significant. One part of Scots culture in which they are significant is in church life, though an all-Scotland religious census does not wholly answer questions about, say, Kelvinside compared to Castlemilk in Glasgow, or of Pilton and Cramond in the same segment of West Edinburgh. It is some help, however, to compare Glasgow – the inner city – with the census unit largely composed of suburbs – Eastwood on the South Side and the northern area of Bearsden, Milngavie, and Strathkelvin.

Yet the different patterns of Protestant church attendance may not diverge as widely as might have been expected – save for a spectacular exception in the Western Isles, Skye and Lochalsh.

Using the census figures, and making some necessarily subjective assumptions about the numbers of the population outside church membership who could be considered as nominal or "sociological" Protestants, I have calculated (see Appendix) the way in which the 507,750 adults and children regularly attending Protestant churches (59% of all church attendance) on any Sunday are divided up as proportions of total "Protestant" population in the different areas of Scotland used for the census. Apart from the Western Isles (52 per cent) the range is not vast – from under 10 per cent in Aberdeen, Dundee, and Lothian outside Edinburgh, to about 15 per cent in Renfrewshire, industrial Lanarkshire and the Glasgow suburbs, and about 16 per cent in the Northern Isles and the main part of the Highlands. Of course these figures inevitably underestimate the number of people who still attend church less regularly, in many cases as communicant members. (For example the Church of Scotland statistics record more than 540,000 members attending Communion in 1983 as against 361,340 attenders, including 95,040 children who were not communicants and adult non-communicant adherents, shown in the census for 1984.)

There are also what might be called enriching divisions in Scotland in so far as regional cultures survive, quite apart from the distinctive place of Gaelic or the wider and less definable characteristics of the Highlands. There is Galloway, which had the strongest Covenanting inheritance, and the Borders. There are those special cases of Orkney and Shetland, and, on a far larger scale, the still distinct and virile regional culture of the North-East – with Aberdeen as its metropolis but by no means limited to Aberdeenshire or Buchan. Yet within this culture, as in the Lowland cities, there are very marked differences of religious style and temperature. To chart all of them one would need a census not by local government areas but by ancient parishes – to bring out, for example, the different moods of Buchan farming communities and their neighbours in the fishing villages of the coast.

The census casts a new light on some of those divisions, though not on others. Its findings need to be interpreted cautiously and sensitively, and with an understanding not only of tradition and ancient customs but of contemporary social changes. By far the most important of these has been what can be interpreted as either the decline or the expansion of Glasgow: the decline in population in the old city limits (as well as of the traditional shipbuilding and engineering industries) and the spread of Glaswegians – especially middle-class and skilled working-class Glaswegians – to the outer suburbs, the towns of the Clyde Valley and Ayrshire coast, and the specially built new towns such as East Kilbride and Cumbernauld. These trends help to explain the relatively weak position of the Church of Scotland in the City of Glasgow, for the exodus has probably drawn away the social groups among whom Protestant church-going remains strongest. And although one result of the exodus has been to spread a stronger Roman Catholic middle-class and professional element over the rest of Scotland, its most emphatic religious result has been to emphasise and to some extent exaggerate the extent to which Roman Catholicism is now the dominant Church in and around Glasgow. Another, hardly obvious in the census, has been to give "Asian" religions an immigrant presence in the inner city – especially in the inner South Side which early in this century was notable for a strong Jewish presence, now largely found in the Renfrewshire suburbs.

The census brings out the extent to which the "Catholic population" (which the RC Church uses for its membership statistics) remains concentrated in the West. It cannot bring out some consequences of that situation which subtly affect attitudes of church-going Protestants, nominal Protestants, and Roman Catholics in East and West. In Edinburgh and the East, by and large, religious adherence is a private, or at least a personal, matter. In Greater Glasgow and the West (especially in parts of industrial Lanarkshire) it is a social, even an ethnic matter. There was an element of truth, as well as of gross exaggeration, in the attitude one sometimes found towards the Papal visit to Scotland in 1982 – that it was the grandest Irish folk festival Scotland had ever seen! (Of course it was also intensely significant that it was possible for that visit to take place, not only with ecumenical courtesies but with a wide measure of goodwill.)

One may debate the significance and implications of this communal divide in the West of Scotland – and a study of either Scottish education or West of Scotland football shows that it is still a divide – but the census both confirms it and conceals it: for it is not only, or nowadays mainly, a division between those who actually go to church or keep their names on a church roll. In places (and not only football grounds) it is more acute among the non-attenders. To be a Protestant in (say) industrial Lanarkshire is not quite the same thing as being a member of a Protestant Church. Nor do denominational differences among Protestants in this situation have even the limited significance that they have in some other parts of Scotland.

This "ethnic" situation is the modern inheritance of the vast Irish immigration of the nineteenth century, when Clydeside was the maritime workshop of the world. The Irish immigration and connection have influenced the moods, styles, and sociology of Protestantism as well as of Roman Catholicism in the area. But historically the Highland connection is at least as important to Glasgow and Clydeside. Gaels came in great numbers, but most of their descendents ceased to be Gaels, even though at the beginning of the industrial revolution Gaelic was still spoken in "frontier" parts of the Highlands that are today within commuting range of Glasgow.

One result of the census is to confirm the other evidence available about the retreat of Gaelic, especially as a first language of community life, including the community of worship. It is not much of an exaggeration to say that it retains that role only in the Outer Hebrides, and that even there it is under challenge – not so much from the powers that be as from the crisis of cultural identity among Gaels themselves, even at worship and in prayer.

Yet there is a Highland character, and there are Highland styles of religious expression, even where Gaelic is no longer the main language of church and community. In several parts of the Hebrides and Highland mainland the "boundaries" of the Protestant majority and Roman Catholic minority remain where they were settled in the age of the Counter-Reformation, with a relaxed social co-existence and a far greater ability to articulate profound theological differences than is generally found among the Rangers or Celtic faithful at Ibrox and Parkhead.

Despite the pressures which modern society imposes, especially on those the census groups together as "Conservative Presbyterians" (mainly the "Wee Frees" and the separate Free Presbyterians), the Highland culture still reflects the religious movements of past centuries; the great evangelisation after the disaster of the Jacobite rebellions, the impact of the 19th-Century Evangelicals and the Disruption of 1843, and the Highland predominance among those Presbyterians who stood aside from the reunion processes which by 1929 had created the Church of Scotland in its modern form.

One must be wary of the results and trends shown in such a census as this where they refer to relatively small areas or denominations; and one must also take into account an uncertainty about how to regard the area around Inverness and firths to the north of it. This is where the Highland culture meets that of the Scots North-East and mingles with it. Despite some setbacks (notably at Invergordon) it has also been one of Scotland's economic growth areas of recent decades, more akin in mood to Orkney, Shetland, and the oil-coast of Aberdeenshire than to other parts of the Highlands and Islands.

But there is still a Highland line, uncertain though the frontier is in places. Beyond it religion probably still counts far more in the life of the people, regardless of communicant membership statistics. Moreover in the Highland Presbyterian Churches – the Church of Scotland in many places as well as the Free Kirk and "FPs" – church membership is quite different in meaning from that of the rest of Presbyterian Scotland. Adult attendance is often far higher than membership, with many regular church-goers remaining "adherents" and becoming full members (if at all) comparatively late in life. Ministers, especially in the Church of Scotland, may deplore the custom and try to change it, but often with indifferent success. It reflects a sense (perhaps exaggerated) of the standard of Christian faith and life Church members must attain. It also fits in with the mixture of relative infrequency and intense solemnity with which this Highland Presbyterianism celebrates the Lord's Supper. The "adherents" (nearly 20 per cent of the adult population in the Western Isles) are not communicants, though in every other respect, including contributions to the Church, they may be more devoted than the majority of people on church rolls elsewhere in Scotland.

The opposite situation may exist in large areas of Eastern Scotland where church rolls are high in proportion to population (especially as "Catholic population" statistics do not account for a large share of membership in these parts of the country). Attendance at church and "Christian giving" do not bear out the promise of the Church statistics.

This could be said of the Borders and indeed much of rural and small town Scotland, but it is perhaps most characteristic of the North-East – always excepting the fishing towns and villages and quite numerous congregations with an evangelical tradition or strong leadership, or both!

In Tayside (Dundee excepted) nearly half of adult Protestants are communicant members; in Grampian (Aberdeen excepted) and the Borders the figure is about 45 per cent. Yet actual Protestant all-age church attendance in these areas is only a little above Glasgow's 12 per cent and below industrial Lanarkshire's 15 per cent – though the figures for adult Protestant church membership (as a percentage of nominal Protestants) is 27 per cent in Glasgow and not above 30 per cent in Motherwell and Monklands.

Yet in parts of the North-East and in the Borders church attendance (or so the census suggests) is scoring against the run of play – *with or without* increasing church membership, even when population movement is taken into account.

At first sight this might link with another regional characteristic of the North-East. The Episcopal Church, though small in numbers, has an encouraging trend in church attendance; and the North-East is the major region where it is most difficult to tag the Episcopalians with the colloquial name for them in some other parts of Scotland: "the English Church". In the North-East Episcopalianism has a Scots tradition going back to the times when it was still uncertain whether the Scots Reformation would produce a purely Presbyterian system or one with a modified version of Episcopacy. But such interpretations must be cautious. The scores against the run of play appear to affect the Church of Scotland too – despite the apparently low evangelical temperature of much of the North-East and the Borders. And the greatest Episcopal strength and attendance growth is in the very different climate of Edinburgh, where it is reasonable to suggest that the native strains of Episcopalianism are substantially diluted or enriched by an English presence. Incidentally, the apparent growth of attendance in what appears (not least in Edinburgh) to be a very middle-class Church with an upper crust seems to raise questions about whether some churchmen worry too much about "middle-class" characteristics in church life.

Or is the lesson of the North-East that a comparatively modest renewal in the church's leadership (from ministers or lay leaders or both) may produce a disproportionate improvement in congregational vigour? Is it easier to revive a church life where the institution retains its place in community life, even when it has seemed weak and apathetic with largely nominal membership, than to create new church growth in areas where (at least among Protestants) most people have no formal church connection?

A census does not answer all the questions it provokes, especially since it is primarily concerned with the statistics of membership and attendance and not the nuances of membership's different meanings and of subjective religious attachment. Opinion polls, such as the BBC/ Sunday Standard System Three one of 1983, find two-thirds of Scots calling themselves Church of Scotland or non-denominationally Protestant, with 18 per cent Roman Catholic, and suggest that belief in God and Jesus Christ as

Son of God runs far ahead of church attendance. Moreover there are different attitudes even within the churches to the importance of perfect attendance. A Church may give the impression it is desirable rather than essential!

But this census does raise many questions, including some more urgent and acute, especially among young people, than such pollsters' findings suggest. They arise in different forms in different parts of a small but still highly regional and varied country.

Sometimes these are the result of distinct local situations, such as the strong Methodist tradition in Shetland (lost from sight among "other denominations" in the census) or the special problems of the Gaelic-speaking churches, which include the particular kind of Gaelic and the style of worship traditionally associated with the language.

Sometimes they are questions raised when impressions created by church vigour and enthusiasm do not seem to be sustained statistically. The Church of Scotland in the last decade has had two major doctrinal cases where its ministers and elders, or a fringe group among them, seemed influenced by Baptist theology: one in the Lanarkshire steel belt, the other in Caithness. Baptists have added to their membership – yet not, it would seem, their church attendance. Nor, for that matter, have the enthusiastic dedicated people one encounters in small independent churches. Indeed the irony of the census is that it shows growth in one church (the Episcopalians) which sets a special value on continuity and traditions (as it interprets them) and in areas where the church as a whole is not at all radical in its theology or restrictive in its definition of membership! There is no sign that intense political commitment or doctrinal firmness (for who could be firmer than the "conservative" Presbyterians?) checks the social and cultural trends which affect both church membership and attendance. The census seems to warn against facile enthusiasm for doctrinal or political formulae for revival, including ecumenical ones.

It also leaves unanswered some questions about the Church of Scotland, which for historical as well as "ideological" reasons seeks the burdens of a national church's territorial ministry, and about the Roman Catholic Church, concentrated for historical reasons in Glasgow and Clydeside. Asked to select the Top Ten religious sites in Scotland – Iona, Whithorn, etc., – a shrewd competitor once added the Broomielaw Quay in Glasgow – "where the Irish landed". The census shows both the scale of the landing and the continuing strength of the revived Roman Catholic Church in Scotland, in community and in devotion – a strength of which the papal visit was an outward and visible symbol. But it also implicitly challenges the view, sometimes encountered among Rome's most fervent supporters and opponents in Scotland, that the Roman Church has a monolithic solidity which will brush aside the half-hearted attempts of the Kirk to affirm or recover its role as the pre-eminent national expression of Scots Christianity. On the contrary, the signs are that the Roman Communion is encountering at least some of the problems of the rest of Scotish Christianity. However, the census figures on their own do not allow anyone to leap to conclusions about the Roman Church in its very different geographical situations – as a powerful ethnic community, as the people's church of parts of the Highlands and Islands, and scattered throughout the rest of Scotland, where it is a minority denomination within the community rather than a distinctive sector of it. Nor can a census of attendance, as distinct from attitudes, yield much fresh evidence about the long-term result of the strain which hard-line clerical attitudes to marriage, divorce, and contraception may impose on many Roman Catholics, especially in the cities and suburbs.

The Roman Catholic concentration and attendance figures help to raise a possibility – here the census trends are suggestive rather than conclusive – that the geographical differences in Scottish patterns of religious life may actually widen. On the face of things one might expect the opposite at a time when Stornoway watches "Dallas" and people whose ancestors sang bothy ballads now know more about the Top Ten.

But the trends which assimilate Edinburgh or Glasgow suburban lifestyles to the patterns of London or Munich, or (as far as climate and economics allow) Los Angeles, may widen the gap with small town, rural, Highland and island Scotland. The Lewis Sabbath may be threatened but it at least maintains the relative gap from the Edinburgh Sunday of golf, shopping, and drinking. The country parishes may complain of thin congregations and ministers scampering from kirk to kirk in their linked parishes; but there is still a church which is a visible part of a recognisable community. It is no longer so in some suburbs, not all of them council-housing estates.

The religious factors in the life of Skye, or Lewis, or Barra, or Morar, or Buckie are not unchanging, but they will remain. Where the church remains as a factor in community life – as the census suggests and evidence in very different parts of Scotland confirms – it can, given the right leadership, be revived.

But what of urban Scotland? Many of the Church of Scotland parishes are not in any sense communities. The other Protestants are gathered congregations. The very strength of the Roman Catholic community in the West creates problems not only of ecumenical relations but of joint mission. The factors which still give strength and cohesion to West of Scotland Roman Catholicism – especially its schools – create divisions not just between churches but between what one may, according to taste, describe as parts of the community or the different communities.

Trends affecting all Western Christendom may in time create a new sense of Christian community within the general community. For some purposes that no doubt already exists. But in much of Scotland – in different styles reflecting history as well as geography – the assumption lingers that the general community is in some sense a Christian one, with church attendance and membership matters of personal taste and choice but without any clear, far less a rigid, fence separating the flock in the pews from the wider Christian fold of Scottish society. Perhaps such an assumption is becoming untenable, at least in urban Scotland. The census evidence is valuable but inconclusive.

APPENDIX: all-age regular Protestant church attendance by districts calculated as an approximate percentage of all Protestants including those with no formal church connection. (National figure approximately 13 to 14 per cent.)

Western Isles, Skye, Lochalsh	52
Shetland	17
Orkney	16
Highland (except Isles etc.)	16
Motherwell and Monklands	15
Renfrew and Inverclyde	15
Eastwood, Bearsden etc.	15
Grampian (except Aberdeen)	14
Dumbarton etc.	13
Ayrshire (Kyle etc.)	13
East Kilbride etc.	13
Dumfries and Galloway	13
Central Scotland	12
Tayside (except Dundee)	12
Glasgow	12
Borders	12
Edinburgh	11
Fife	10
Lothian (except Edinburgh)	9
Aberdeen	9
Dundee	9

SIZE AND GROWTH

Rev PETER BISSET
*Warden, St. Ninian's
Centre, Crieff*

It was a daunting assignment to be invited to prepare a commentary on the findings of the MARC survey as they related to the size and growth of the churches in Scotland. Too often, it seemed, it had been my unhappy task to focus the attention of the Church which I serve upon the statistics of decline which have marked the major part of the last thirty years, and which, at times, I suspected were not being treated with the seriousness they deserved.

That these trends were serious I was in no doubt. A membership decline of approximately 30% could not easily be dismissed as of no consequence. What was even more serious was that the decline in communion attendance as recorded by congregations showed a fall of some 40% over the corresponding period. Since this figure perhaps reflected more accurately the practising membership of the Kirk it appeared that the statistics of decline did not simply record a process whereby the Kirk shed from its Rolls those who were nonpractising members. To the contrary, it appeared that membership decline reflected a real loss, as not only did the Kirk fail to maintain its membership through recruitment of new communicants, but lost from its membership through a process of 'falling away'.

Although my observation of these trends related particularly to the Church of Scotland, there was every reason to believe that similar trends had been evidenced in the other denominations, and none had emerged from these years unscathed.

The tragedy of decline was highlighted in my thinking even more by the fact that the falling away had occurred after a period of real missionary advance in the post war decade. During this period the Church of Scotland, as well as other churches in varying degree, had seen a significant expansion of its membership, and had experienced an unprecedented responsiveness to its ministry and mission. The fact that the falling away, when it occurred, observably coincided with years of dramatic social and cultural change was not in itself sufficient explanation. If the Church's membership was to be affected so drastically by its experience of changing times, then there had to be real question marks placed over the period of advance. Had the gains been real? What did membership mean if members so swiftly fell away in less encouraging times?

These were, and are, real questions. They are, of course, easily answered by simple reference to the Parable of the Sower. There is the seed which falls on shallow soil, and has a shortlived life, just as there is the seed which falls amidst thorns, and growth is soon inhibited by a less than congenial environment. These facts of experience have to be given due weight, as the warning of Our Lord has to be heard, but the comment of the farmer upon the parable

perhaps also has to be heeded. "It could only happen once!" There are lessons to be learned. There is action to be taken if we are concerned for growth.

Inevitably, these thirty years have been years of questioning. Self-examination has been real as the churches have sought to come to terms with the experience of a new age ruthlessly exposing inadequacies of faith and fellowship. Few congregations have not experienced the rigours of re-appraisal and questioned whether the Church as we have known it might not be in process of disappearing to allow a new form of Church to appear which would be more adequate for vastly changing times. Indeed, at times, it appeared that the future might lie with the 'little flocks' rather that the big battalions, and the vitality of the Church's life be found in smaller fellowship groupings rather than in large congregations. That judgement has been made at times on the basis of new discoveries of faith within the intimacy of fellowship of such groups. At times it has been the judgement of those who, in despondency, witnessed the disappearance of once busy churches.

What has been gained in such discovery must not be lost. Indeed, there is wide evidence from world experience that growing churches are churches which have given place within their life for such experience of fellowship in which the life of faith can become intimately and vitally alive.

It was, however, in this land of the Covenant, a near betrayal to think of a Scotland in which there would not be a Church which hoisted high the flag of faith at the heart of the nation's life, and summoned a nation to the obedience of the King of kings.

The statistics of this survey do much to suggest that those who have written off the Church in Scotland's story have been hasty in their judgement. Indeed, there is much in these pages to suggest that the Church is still a formidable force in Scotland's story, and that the Church which is now emerging with new vitality may, indeed, be a Church which has been strengthened through the years of self-examination and re-appraisal.

Small signs have been there over the last decade for those who have eyes to see. There has been evidence that the steep slide of decline has been halted. There have been signs of a new responsiveness where the Church was ready to respond to it. At last there is available a body of statistical evidence to confirm these signs, and no branch of the Chistian Church in Scotland can afford to ignore the picture which this mass of figures begins to present.

In contrast to some other areas of the United Kingdom, Scotland can still claim almost half of the adult population within the recorded membership of the churches.

Fig 1 Proportion of population who are church members

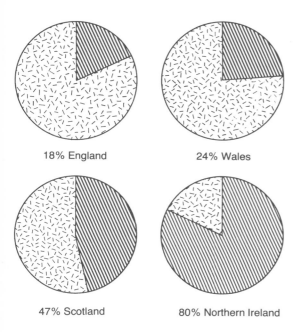

18% England   24% Wales

47% Scotland   80% Northern Ireland

Fig 2   Areas of growth & decline in adult church attendance 1980-1984

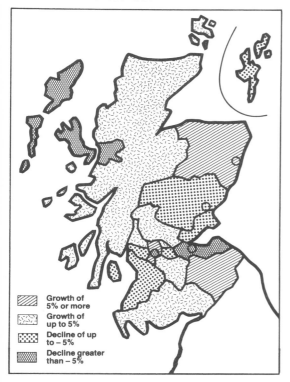

Growth of 5% or more
Growth of up to 5%
Decline of up to − 5%
Decline greater than − 5%

These figures must, of course, be treated with some caution since the Roman Catholic membership figure includes children, a practice which is not paralleled in the other denominations. Likewise, any general census of church affiliation within the land would most probably produce statistics at a much higher level, and this fact also has some relevance for the Church's mission.

More importantly, however, it is some sign of the vitality of the Church in Scotland that one in six of the adult population is at worship each Sunday. What other body could rival these statistics?

True, these figures represent a 5% fall in Church membership over the period of the survey, but the fact that Church attendance declined only by 2% suggests the emergence of a more committed membership, a hopeful pointer to the future. The hopefulness of this statistic is emphasised by the fact that in certain areas, notably the Borders and Dumfries and Galloway, attendance is showing a marked increase while membership remains in decline.

This fact is the more striking when it is reckoned that previous indicators would have suggested the south as the least likely area of the country to show signs of growth. It is not an area which has been affected greatly by population change or growth, and many would have judged that there was in the south a settled somnolence which would not readily show signs of awakening.

Even more significantly, while the percentage of young people in the population has fallen by 8%, the decline in Church attendance among this age group is only 3%. It would appear that the Church in Scotland is managing to retain its young people to a marked degree. This fact may well be the more important when it is recalled that it was the exodus of young people from Sunday School in the late fifties which gave signal of the decline in membership which was soon to affect the whole Church. Again, the Borders register significantly, where in spite of a fall in the child population of 6%, child attendance at Church rose by 8%. Central Region shows a similar trend with a gain of 6% in face of a child population decline of 6%.

If these statistics give cautious hope for the future, they may also raise real questions regarding the shape of that future. The ecumenical debate has over the years suggested that the denominational shape of the Church must alter if the Church is to enter the 21st century with relevance and realism. That debate left Scotland largely untouched. Your true Scot knew that the shape of the Church was Presbyterian! That conviction was a matter of cultural identity as much as religious persuasion. It was a product of history and the consequence of the shaping of a nation. Depth of feeling attached to Presbyterian principle which had little to do with Christian piety. Hence the anathema with which the country reacted in one historic moment when in unity conversations with the Church of England it was proposed that there might be bishops in the Kirk!

If the Church of Scotland has seemed willing at times to relinquish, at least in part, these proud principles, there were certainly other branches of the Presbyterian family which would have risen in protest to ensure that the true face of Christ's Kirk in Scotland was not despoiled! It is perhaps some evidence of the peculiar strength of Presbyterianism in Scotland that other denominations have not figured prominently in the spectrum of church allegiance. The Scottish Episcopal Church, which alone of the smaller denominations registers over 1% of the population within its membership, has been largely suspect as historically at least it was identified with the landed gentry; while the Roman Catholic Church, which alone beside the National Church claimed a sizeable section of the population, was clearly seen as deriving its main strength from the immigrant Irish community. In culture, the Kirk was surely 'established' in Scottish society.

Times are, however, a-changing. It is now the Roman Catholic Church which can boast the highest number of adult worshippers in Scotland (287,000), with the Church of Scotland lagging slightly behind (266,000). Significantly it is the stricter Presbyterian churches which appear to be most in decline, and the Scotish Episcopal Church, bishops notwithstanding, which can claim an attendance increase of 9%.

Proud Presbyterianism may well tremble! The figures may, of course, be misleading. The Roman Catholic Church has, indeed, maintained its strength to a greater degree than the Church of Scotland, and has probably gained from the strong sense of identity built up through unhappy years when it was looked upon as an alien body in the land. It has also gained from the control it retains over its young people through its own school system. For all of that its strength continues to lie in the west where it can claim a considerable percentage of the adult population within its membership. The following figures exclude estimated Catholic child membership:

	R C	Protestant
Strathclyde: Motherwell and Monklands	36%	21%
Strathclyde: Dumbarton, Clydesdale, Cumbernauld and Kilsyth	34%	19%
Strathclyde: Renfrew & Inverclyde	29%	25%
Strathclyde: Glasgow	29%	16%
Strathclyde: Eastwood, Bearsden etc.	22%	22%
Strathclyde: East Kilbride, etc.	20%	24%
Strathclyde: Kyle and Carrick, etc.	12%	30%

These figures show the Roman Catholic community in the west extending its boundaries and establishing even more firmly its dominance in the region.

Beyond the Church of Scotland and the Roman Catholic Church, the statistics of the smaller denominations represent such a small percentage of the total that they must be handled with care. The Conservative Presbyterian churches have registered a high degree of decline (10%).

The real truth is, of course, that the strength of these churches has lain in the more remote areas of the Highlands and Islands where they have effectively safeguarded a way of life and a discipline of faith which have not been eroded to the same degree as has been the case for other churches more exposed to the pressures of secular society and social revolution. Even the remotest Hebridean island is not now immune from these influences, and with growing populations both in the Highlands and Islands the Conservative Presbyterian Churches face a challenge which will test their ability to hold fast to conviction but adapt to changing times.

It is in the East, in Lothian and Tayside, and particularly in the City of Edinburgh, that the Scottish Episcopal Church has made its most impressive advances, although once again the numbers involved are not so great as to alter significantly the denominational picture.

On the face of it, it appears that the ecclesiastical face of Scotland is little altered. Indeed, it must appear to many of the smaller denominations that their place within the religious spectrum is closely akin to that of the smaller political parties who must at times wonder whether they can ever escape from the dominance of the two party system!

A contrast of the growth patterns of the various denominations is, however, illuminating.

Overall the churches saw an overall decrease in membership and attendance of 3% and 2% respectively. The spread of this decline appears as follows:

Fig 3 Percentage membership change 1980-1984

Within the attendance figures another pattern, however, emerges:

Fig 4 Percentage change 1980-1984 of adult and child attendance

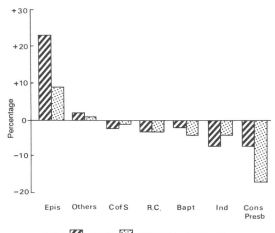

Adult ▨ & child ▨ attendance growth rate

It is interesting to review the experience of the churches in the light of the thesis propounded by Dean M Kelley in his survey of the denominations in the U S A. Under the title *Why Conservative Churches are Growing* Kelley examines the varying fortunes of the churches in terms of the assertion that religion has to do with meaning, and it is those churches which most convincingly offer 'meaning' which can command the highest degree of commitment, and consequently enjoy the greatest degree of growth.

Kelley has expressed his unhappiness with the title of his book, wished on him by his publishers. He is anxious to insist that the criterion central to his thesis is strictness rather than conservatism and it may only be incidental that within the American experience the criterion of strictness is most applicable to the conservative churches which are, in fact, the growing churches.

It is difficult to apply this criterion simplistically to the Scottish scene. There is no compelling evidence to suggest that strictness in itself is a recipe for growth, although there is every reason to believe that a church which through its ministry and mission enables people to make sense of their world and their life within it may well be able to attract the loyalty of its members and the attention of its world.

In these terms it becomes important to consider not only the standpoint of a church in terms of its doctrine and discipline, but the awareness with which it responds to the needs of its times, and the sensitivity with which it speaks to the problems and perplexities of its age.

When the Church advanced in Scotland during the decade beginning in the mid-forties, it is difficult to believe that its advance was not affected profoundly by the longing widely experienced throughout the land to journey forward into a new day of hope. Coupled with that yearning there was on the part of the churches a serious intent to meet the needs and the challenge of the hour with a ministry and mission which spoke relevantly to a new situation. The commission of the Church of Scotland which sought 'God's Will for Church and Nation' in that crucial hour was symptomatic of that concern.

There is reason to believe that the decline of the churches from the mid-fifties onwards was associated with a mood of disenchantment, and a sense of the inadequacies of traditional religion amidst the complexities of life in the mid-twentieth century. If today there is evidence of a halting of decline and some new readiness for religion it may be useful to assess the experience of the churches in terms of the issues raised by Kelley.

It is the Baptist Church which has shown the most apparent growth in terms of membership. A 4% increase was recorded over the period of the survey, and the increased membership is reflected in most regions. Surprisingly membership gains are not matched by growth in attendance where a 4% decline is recorded – a rate which is 1% higher than the average for all of the churches.

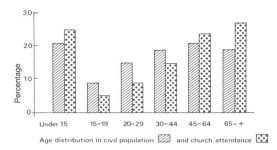

Fig 5 1984 proportions of church attendance and the civil population by age

Age distribution in civil population ▨ and church attendance ⬚

There is little doubt but that the membership growth recorded by the Baptist Union reflects the energy with which they have called their churches over recent years to the concerns of Church Growth, and in terms of Church Growth analysis it might appear that the growth they have experienced has been within the fringe of their 'attenders' without any real penetration in mission into the world around. This understanding is particularly tempting since the Baptist Church of all the churches registers an attendance at worship greater than membership, and in these terms could be seen both as a church where strictness is evident in terms of membership demand, and yet missionary opportunity is apparent in terms of the uncommitted attenders who are a first target for evangelism. For the Baptist Church, as for most of the smaller denominations, the real problem for effective evangelism will lie in reaching beyond the fringe of interest to the wider community in which the norm for religion is determinedly Presbyterian.

The areas of opportunity for The Baptist Union appear to lie particularly in the North East where in Grampian attendance figures still record gains beyond increases in membership. In Shetland and Central Region there is the same encouraging trend to spur forward the missionary endeavour to which the denomination has committed itself. The areas of the north are perhaps particularly significant for the Baptists since population growth in the region related to the oil industry provides room for advance beyond the boundaries of cultural conservatism!

The figures for the Scottish Episcopal Church record a rather different story. While their membership has fallen by 3% (the average rate of decline) attendance has risen by 9% with a staggering increase of 23% in child attendance. The areas of particular growth correspond with those in which the Baptist Union have been making progress. Grampian, Central and Shetland are significant areas of gain while Edinburgh and the Lothians also show strong signs of advance. In addition Fife, Dundee and Orkney are promising growth areas.

Obviously some of the reasons and opportunities for growth correspond with those adduced for the Baptist Church, but, in addition, it may be questioned whether the gains within Lothian do not reflect a cultural acceptability which allows the mission of the Church to go forward in that region.

With regard to the attendance growth evidenced by the Other Denominations (Methodist, Salvation Army etc.) it is difficult to hazard any judgements in view of the number of small groupings which make up this statistic. It is perhaps worthy of note, that the Other Demoninations show evidences of strong growth both in Aberdeen and Lothian where the smaller denominations appear to grow as the Church of Scotland and Roman Catholic Church continue in decline.

It is perhaps the quality of credibility which will most affect the growth of the Church and the advance of its mission in the testing times in which we live particularly after years of consistent decline.
Pointers to credibility may be found in two areas.

Firstly, it might be judged to be a measure of the Church's credibility that it can claim the loyalty of its young people. This has been the traditional stance of the churches which practice infant baptism, but it would certainly be the intent of every church to see its young people growing up in the faith of their parents.

It has already been noted that one source of real hope for the churches is that the decline in Child Attendance of 3% is less than the overall decline of 8% within this segment of the population. There is hope here that the Church in Scotland is managing to retain its young people.

A table contrasting the experience of the various denominations may, however, be helpful in any further evaluation of these statistics.

Child attendance	Change	% of Membership	% of Adult Attendance
Scottish Episcopal	+23%	11%	26%
Other Denominations	+2%	32%	43%
Baptist	−2%	39%	36%
Church of Scotland	−3%	10%	36%
Roman Catholic	−3%	8%	24%
Independent	−7%	35%	46%
Conservative Presbyterian	−8%	16%	23%

These figures should be assessed in relation to the statistic of 27% which represents the ratio of this age group to the adult population. Low percentages will tend to reflect either ageing congregations or a failure of the Church concerned to incorporate young people into its fellowship.

Since Roman Catholic membership figures engross children obviously the 8% noted is not a trustworthy figure, but the 24% in relation to attendance gives cause for concern amidst a section of the population where the child population might be reasonably assessed as near the general figure.

The Church of Scotland and Scottish Episcopal figures likewise give cause for concern, pointing to a real failure in incorporation, aggravated in the case of the Episcopal Church by the low percentage in relation to attendance. The promising gains of the Episcopal Church in this area must accordingly be seen as an advance towards a healthier church certainly as it relates to the young people whom it will hope to embrace within its communicant membership.

The statistics of the Conservative Presbyterian Churches suggest that the serious decline they are presently experiencing may well be located in a failure to embrace their young people within the fellowship of faith and similar trends are apparent in the case of the Independents. It is notably the Baptists, Independents and Other Demoninations which claim statistics which point to a high degree of faithfulness in the incorporation of their young people, but if the attendance figures of the Church of Scotland relate to the committed membership of that church then the 36% attendance may well indicate a strengthening at this level of the Church's life.

The serious pointer to credibility possibly relates to the percentage of a Church's official membership which is actually present at worship. The percentages here indicated make an interesting contrast which in some measure relates to the previous discussion.

Baptist	107%
Independent	76%
Other Denominations	75%
Conservative Presbyterian	68%
Scottish Episcopal	40%
Roman Catholic	35%
Church of Scotland	29%

It is obvious from the denominations at the head of the list that there is some relation between the measure of commitment within a congregation and its effectiveness in incorporating its young people, although the current experience of the Conservative Presbyterians may match the experience of other churches which have found that the erosion of faith among its young people was the first sign of decline.

In that connection it may be significant to compare the distribution of various age groupings in Church and Community (see Fig. 5).

The chart clearly reflects the loss which the churches have experienced over the past thirty years, with the consequent imbalance of older people within their membership.

The challenge in these terms is real. Can the churches move towards a standard of commitment within their membership which will allow young and old to make common cause for Christ and the Gospel? It is here that credibility becomes in a real sense a vital issue for the hour if churches are to speak compellingly to a bewildered world.

The issue is specially crucial for those denominations which record low statistics of attendance. If they cannot command the loyalty of their members, how far can they be expected to win their young people and mobilise their energies in the service of Christ?

It may be wrong, and even misleading, however, to think of these issues denominationally. Loyalty within Protestantism, at least, will tend to be seen in terms of loyalty to a particular fellowship, and membership will tend to lapse where the fellowship is failing to encourage and inspire such loyalty. Indeed, perhaps the greatest encouragement to loyal membership is a sense of belonging to a church which is 'on the move', just as the greatest discouragement is belonging to a congregation where there is little sense of purposeful endeavour, or at worst a desperate sense that congregational effort is directed unavailingly to survival.

Perhaps the most encouraging facet of this survey is its finding that 45% of all Protestant churchgoers in Scotland belong to churches which have grown in significant degree over the period of the survey.

Since the churches record an overall decline in attendance it is apparent that the 22% of congregations which record decreasing attendance are declining faster than the 26% which are growing.

Here is obviously a significant area of enquiry for the churches. How can growth be encouraged and sustained where it is evident? How can static churches be encouraged to move forward? What are the reasons for decline where this is apparent within a particular congregation?

Obviously the answer to these questions will vary from denomination to denomination, as well as region to region. But there is one aspect of the survey's findings which holds a peculiar significance for those in church leadership who seek to plan for the advance of the Church's mission.

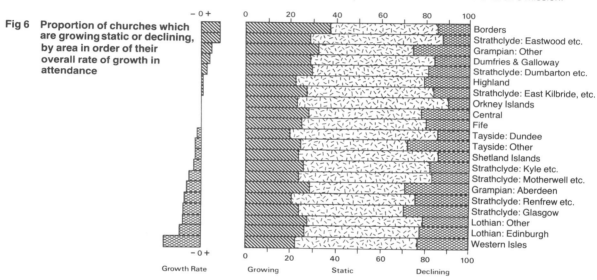

Fig 6 Proportion of churches which are growing static or declining, by area in order of their overall rate of growth in attendance

The distribution of growing churches throughout the regions is shown in Figure 6. (For a definition of 'growing', see article by Peter Brierley – 'Methodology, Notes and Definitions'.) From this table it becomes apparent that the degree of growth within a region depends as much upon the number which are growing, although there is perceptible evidence that a growth situation in any region will depend upon the number of growing churches.

The distribution of growing congregations among the denominations is also of interest. Denominations are here listed in order of the percentage of growing churches.

The survey shows clearly that the congregation of a growing Protestant Church will be much larger than that of a static or declining one. The figures as they relate to the various denominations reveal the following picture.

	Growth	Static	Decline
Baptists	38%	52%	10%
Church of Scotland	29%	41%	30%
Scottish Episcopal	27%	65%	8%
Other Denominations	26%	65%	9%
Roman Catholic	20%	56%	24%
Independent	18%	71%	11%
Conservative Presbyterian	14%	72%	14%
Overall	26%	52%	22%

Average congregation	Growing	Static	Declining	All
Church of Scotland	234	139	74	149
Conservative Presbyterian	108	46	47	59
Scottish Episcopal	102	46	44	52
Baptist	154	89	61	117
Independent	110	63	51	61
Other Denominations	68	47	48	58
All Protestant Churches	182	90	69	108

The inference is obvious. Growing churches within Protestantism are markedly larger, and declining churches much smaller than average. Is there any evidence here that the growing churches have moved beyond the struggle for maintenance which is almost invariably the lot of the small fellowship battling for survival, intent upon the preservation of its buildings and anxious for its future?

There is, however, another fascinating constituent of this analysis. It is probable that 150 is the peak level to which a one-man ministry can carry a congregation. It is notable that the average worshipping congregation of the Church of Scotland is precisely at this level, and growing congregations significantly rising above it. Perhaps it is the Kirk which must be most conscious of this fact since its traditional one-man ministry with the jealous insistence of congregations upon 'having our own man' may be an inhibition upon growth. It is certainly one of the promising signs of the emerging situation within the Kirk that there is a growing awareness of the essential role of the eldership within a Presbyterian system, and a developing conviction that only ministry shared by elders and minister together can carry the Kirk forward.

One pertinent observation in this regard relates to Grampian where the Church of Scotland in a situation of population growth can point to a gratifying increase of 17% in membership. The fact that this increase exceeds the population increase by 10% is encouraging. The fact that recorded attendance has only advanced by 2% is perhaps symptomatic of the problems which beset the Kirk.

The Roman Catholic Church exhibits a similar pattern in relation to growth within its churches. The comparison illustrates the similarities.

	Growing	Static	Declining	All
Average Protestant Congregation	182	90	69	108
Average Roman Catholic Congregation	576	516	392	474

These figures while revealing a similar pattern, also relate to a different situation. The pattern for the Roman Catholic Church involves larger congregations with team ministries and fewer church buildings. The following figures represent the situation reporting for each denomination the number of Attenders, Members and Churches served by one minister.

Church	Attenders	Members	Churches
Roman Catholic	254	721	0.5
Church of Scotland	181	618	1.2
All Others	90	129	1.4

It is difficult to deduce other than that the Roman Catholic Church is deploying its resources to better effect than the fragmented churches of Protestantism, or that the National Church with its heritage of buildings so often bears witness to the schisms and reunions of yesterday rather than strategic response to the needs and opportunities of today.

It is, of course, the needs of today which should form the missionary agenda of the Churches, and that agenda becomes the more apparent when it is reckoned that while one in six of the adult population are in Church on Sunday, the other five are not.

The statistics of church attendance indicate that while 17% of the population are in church on a Sunday, obviously 83% are not. The age distribution of the 4 million who do not attend is as follows:

Under 15	81%	(88%)
15 – 19	87%	(89%)
20 – 29	87%	(92%)
30 – 44	85%	(92%)
45 – 64	82%	(81%)
65 and over	77%	(88%)

The bracketed figures relate to the English situation, and give a basis for comparison. The missionary task facing the churches is formidable. It should, however, be remembered that possibly twice the number of those attending are in fact, in membership of the churches, and a considerable section of the population outside the recorded membership would still judge itself as in some way 'connected' to the church. This is the base for mission in Scotland with the firm resource of a considerable section of the population in active membership of the churches. Perhaps, the statistics only emphasise once again the credibility which is required of the churches if their mission is to advance. That credibility will relate variously to the various strands of the denominational mix which makes up the Church of Jesus Christ in Scotland. It will embrace the firmness of the Christian conviction evidenced by the churches, the degree of commitment of their members, the concern they evidence for the society of which they are a part, and the cultural acceptability of the ethos they represent.

It all amounts to saying that these are renewed days of opportunity for the churches in Scotland. By and large the old loyalties of Kirk and Chapel persist in varying degrees in different regions, but culturally the winds of change are producing a situation in which traditions will only survive if they relate with relevance to new situations and new needs. Within that situation there are possibilities for advance for many of the smaller denominations as they demonstrate vitality of faith and consistency of Christian witness. Scotland today needs once again to see the fair face of Christ in the churches.

Fig 7 Christian allegiance by area

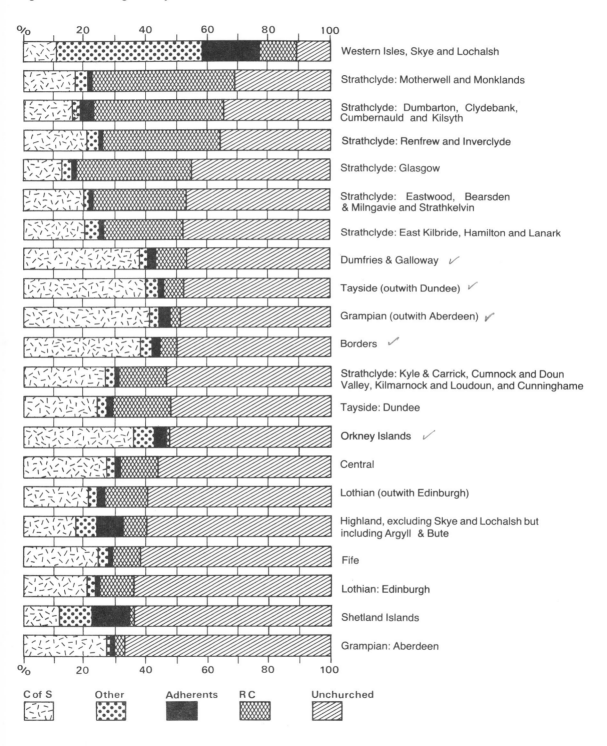

| | C of S | Other | Adherents | R C | Unchurched |

25

BIBLE USE IN THE SCOTTISH CHURCHES

Dr JOHN DRANE
Lecturer in New Testament in the Department of Religious Studies at the University of Stirling

1 Introduction

1.1   One section of the census form asked for information about use of the Bible in the Scottish churches. Two major questions concern us here:
– Which version is most often read˙ publicly during Sunday services?
– Which version would normally be used in the context of a (less formal) mid-week Bible study group?
In answer to these questions, a number of alternative versions were offered: Authorised Version (AV), New English Bible (NEB), Good News Bible (GNB), New International Version (NIV), Jerusalem Bible (JER), Revised Standard Version (RSV), and Others (which in fact accounted for a very small percentage of the total).

1.2   These two apparently simple questions raise a number of other issues. For as well as providing straightforward factual information, the answers to them can also be reformulated in such a way as to relate them to other aspects of the survey. For example:
– Is there any correlation between growing or declining churches and the versions of the Bible that they use?
– Do churches which take Bible study seriously enough to hold a mid-week meeting for this purpose find that some versions are more amenable to practical Bible use than others?
– Is there any connexion between geography/social context and the use of different Bible versions?

1.3   For those concerned with the use of the Bible in the churches, and our future strategy in Scotland, these are all crucial questions. The census has gone some way to providing answers. But it has to be admitted at the outset that these answers are far from clearcut: not only do they vary from region to region, but they are in some senses mutually contradictory.

2 The Versions and the Churches

2.1   With two exceptions, it is not possible to make a simple identification of particular churches with particular versions. In practice, each denomination generally uses more than one version. Quite often, the same congregation will use more than one version: a Sunday version and a mid-week version. The exceptions are the Roman Catholic church, where the Jerusalem Bible is universally used (with only minimal use of others on a generally informal basis); and the Conservative Presbyterians, who use the AV almost exclusively. The table below summarises the actual use of the different versions by each denomination. A number of factors are worth noting here.

2.2   *The dominance of the AV.* In the national figures for all churches, it is surprising to see that the AV is still the dominant version in use in Protestant churches, both on Sundays and in mid-week Bible study groups. Of all those who go to church in Scotland, 28% regularly hear the

Bible Version used in Church

	Church of Scot	Cons Pres	Scottish Episcopal	Baptist	Indep	Others	Total Protestant	Roman Catholic	Total
AV	33%	92%	47%	27%	70%	62%	47%	1%	40%
GNB	29%	½%	20%	15%	11%	23%	24%	0%	20%
JER	0%	0%	26%	0%	0%	1%	1%	94%	15%
NEB	36%	0%	46%	3%	9%	12%	27%	0%	23%
NIV	7%	4%	2%	53%	20%	13%	11%	0%	9%
RSV	20%	½%	39%	33%	12%	16%	19%	5%	17%
Others	3%	3%	4%	2%	2%	4%	3%	1%	3%
Percentage of churches on which figures are based	82%	68%	59%	69%	56%	83%	76%	69%	75%

Percentages sum to more than 100% because some churches use more than one version.

Authorised Version. This cuts across denominational boundaries, though the Conservative Presbyterians use it most (92%), followed closely by Independents (70%) and Others (62%). But a third of Church of Scotland congregations use it, and almost half the Episcopalians. Baptists use it less than any other single Protestant denomination, but even there more than a quarter of Baptist churches use the AV, while in several areas it is the dominant Sunday version among Baptists (see the various regional statistics). With the possible exception of the Conservative Presbyterians, it must be many generations since clergy were trained on the basis of the AV. Its persistence in the churches on such a large scale only serves to highlight the acknowledged gap between theological education and the day-to-day work of local congregations. It also suggests that choice of Bible version is often related not to intelligibility but to aesthetic and social conventions.

2.3 *The relative decline of the RSV.* The RSV is now less popular than it once was. In the national figures it does not feature at all as the favourite version of any denomination for either Sunday or midweek use. (See table of Scotland totals.) It is clear that churches are now either staying with the Authorised Version or abandoning the AV/RV/RSV lineage altogether in favour of one of the more recent modern translations. Only 17% of all churches now use the RSV for any purpose, the greatest loyalty to it being in the Scottish Episcopal Church – though even here, only 39% of congregations use it and in no area of the country does it emerge as the main or only version. Nevertheless, in terms of church attendance, 14% of all worshippers will hear it read regularly.

2.4 *Bibles by denomination.* Notwithstanding what has been said in 2.1 above, one of the most striking features to emerge from the survey is the way that particular versions have become identified with specific denominations in Scotland.

2.4a *The Jerusalem Bible* is used by 94% of Roman Catholics, but by virtually no-one else. The reason for this is not hard to find, as it is the only version authorised for regular Sunday use in the Roman Catholic church. Because of this consistency of usage, it is in fact the most widely used version of all, with 37% of all church-goers hearing it regularly.

2.4b *The Authorised Version* is almost the only version used by Conservative Presbyterians, and by a large majority of Independents. Some Independents in particular probably use it (like many Church of Scotland congregations) for reasons related to custom and tradition

(which also certainly explains its continuing widespead use by Conservative Presbyterians).

2.4c *The New English Bible* is the next most widely used major version, with 16% of all church attenders hearing it regularly. Almost half the Scottish Episcopal congregations use it, and it is the single most popular version in regular use in the Church of Scotland, especially for Sunday services. This popularity could well be related to historical factors. The Presbytery of Dunblane was instrumental in inaugurating the translation of the NEB, and the Church of Scotland (along with the English churches) played a major role in its production.

2.4d *The New International Version* is most popular with Baptists, with over half using it for Sunday worship and for all mid-week meetings. The reason for this is probably theological rather than denominational as such, for the NIV is also popular among many Independent churches (together with a much smaller number of Church of Scotland and Scottish Episcopal congregations). The NIV was originally produced as an 'evangelical' option to other (supposedly 'liberal') modern versions, and the conservative position of its translators no doubt reflects the views of many Baptists. This must certainly be the major factor in explaining why the NIV is the only modern version with any sort of following at all among Conservative Presbyterians. But this denominational bias needs to be put into perspective. Overall, the NIV is the least popular version in the Scottish churches, with only 6% of church-goers regularly using it. It is of course a relatively recent publication.

2.4e *The Good News Bible* is most popular in the Church of Scotland and the Scottish Episcopal Church, generally for use in mid-week meetings. But it is in fact more widely used than the national figures may seem to suggest, with 14% of all church attenders hearing it regularly. In addition, the churches in a number of key geographical areas use it very extensively. It is the favourite Sunday and mid-week version in Aberdeen, and in two districts of Strathclyde (Renfrew and Inverclyde; and Eastwood, Bearsden, Milngavie and Strathkelvin). It also appears as the most used study Bible in Grampian region, Fife, Lothian, Dundee and Glasgow, with significant use in other districts of Strathclyde and in Highland region (for which see the various regional statistics).

3. **Bible Versions and Church attendance**

3.1 There is some evidence to suggest that the Bible version used on a Sunday varies with the size of the church, as the following table illustrates.

Size of 1984 Church attendance:	Less than 50	50-149	150-249	250-399	400 or more	Overall
AV	58%	50%	45%	43%	7%	40%
GNB	13%	19%	20%	21%	8%	20%
JER	7%	8%	8%	9%	69%	15%
NEB	18%	21%	24%	24%	9%	23%
NIV	8%	10%	10%	10%	2%	9%
RSV	15%	18%	18%	18%	10%	17%
Others	3%	3%	3%	3%	0%	3%
Percentage of churches	33%	34%	15%	8%	10%	100%

3.2 In the smallest churches, the AV tends to dominate. But as attendance figures rise, the use of the AV diminishes, and there is a corresponding rise in the popularity of the NEB and GNB, up to the 400 mark. At that point the Jerusalem Bible assumes dominance – a feature that reflects the generally larger attendance at Roman Catholic churches (nearly all the largest churches in Scotland are RC).

3.3 It would be tempting to suggest that larger congregations are attracted by the use of modern versions like the NEB, GNB, or Jerusalem Bible. But this equation cannot be made on the basis of these figures. The figures themselves are just another way of expressing denominational preferences in use of Bible versions. We have already noted (2.4b) that the heaviest users of the AV are the Conservative Presbyterians, Independents and Others. Closer analysis of the figures relating to these groups shows that a significant number of the churches in these three categories have attendances of less than 149, and many of them have less than 50. Church size and Bible version are not therefore related in any meaningful way. To make such a correlation would require evidence of congregations which had increased in size as a result of turning from use of the AV to a modern version. The census form did not ask such retrospective questions, and it is not possible to extrapolate and answer from the figures relating merely to attendance and Bible version.

4 Bible Versions and Church Growth

4.1 Can we differentiate between growing churches, declining churches, and those which remain static, on the basis of the Bible versions they use? The following table indicates how the versions relate to these categories of churches in the various denominations.

	Congregations which were :		
	Growing	Static	Declining
Church of Scotland	NEB	AV	AV
Conservative Presbyterian	AV	AV	AV
Scottish Episcopal	NEB	AV	AV/NEB
Baptist	NIV	NIV	NIV
Independent	AV	AV	AV
Other Denominations	AV	AV	AV
Roman Catholic	JER	JER	JER

With the possible exception of the figures from the Church of Scotland, there is nothing at all here to indicate that Bible version as such is directly related to church growth or decline. However, it must be of some significance that the three denominations with the highest percentage of growing churches (Church of Scotland, Scottish Episcopal Church, and Baptists) all use predominantly modern versions – while the churches with the fastest rate of decline (Conservative Presbyterians) are the most firmly entrenched in their commitment to the AV. But it is unclear whether there is any direct and simple correlation between these two factors. In the fastest growing denominations, growth, decline and Bible version all vary from region to region, and within any given area a particular version can be used by churches in any category (see the tables of regional statistics).

4.2 This comes out more clearly if we consider the overall national position of church life in relation to Bible versions used:

	Growing churches	Static churches	Declining churches	Overall
AV	32%	46%	35%	40%
GNB	22%	17%	22%	20%
JER	13%	16%	16%	15%
NEB	29%	20%	23%	23%
NIV	12%	9%	6%	9%
RSV	20%	17%	15%	17%
Others	3%	2%	3%	3%
Percentage of churches	26%	52%	22%	100%

It is immediately obvious from this that every version can be associated with both growth and decline! There is no direct statistical link here between church growth and Bible version, though there may well be more subtle indicators once the statistics are placed in a broader interpretative framework (see section 6 below). No doubt many factors are involved in a proper analysis of the phenomenon of church growth (not least, social and geographical considerations). But so far as the Bible is concerned, the major and most obvious conclusion to emerge is that church growth is related not so much to which version is used, as to *how* it is used and applied to the local church situation.

5 Bible Versions and mid-week meetings

5.1 What is the relationship between churches using one version on Sunday and the same or another midweek? This is indicated in the table below, where the totals have been deliberately constrained to add up to 100% for simplicity. This table shows the overall use of Bible versions in midweek and on Sundays. Thus reading across, the AV line for

Bible Versions used on Sunday and Midweek

		Midweek							
		AV	GNB	JER	NEB	NIV	RSV	Other	Total
Sunday	AV	19%	3%	0%	3%	2%	1%	1%	29%
	GNB	2%	11%	0%	1%	2%	1%	0%	17%
	JER	0%	2%	5%	1%	0%	1%	0%	9%
	NEB	2%	3%	0%	9%	0%	1%	0%	15%
	NIV	2%	1%	0%	0%	7%	1%	0%	11%
	RSV	2%	3%	1%	1%	1%	8%	0%	16%
	Other	1%	1%	0%	0%	0%	0%	1%	3%
	Total	28%	24%	6%	15%	12%	13%	2%	100%

example has a total of 29%. This indicates that 29% of churches use the AV on Sundays. Reading vertically, the AV column has a total of 28%. This indicates that 28% of churches use the AV mid-week. Where the AV line and column cross is the figure of 19%. This means 19% of churches use the AV mid-week *and* on Sundays. The 3% next to the 19% on the AV line in the GNB column means that 3% of churches use the AV on Sundays and GNB mid-week. The 2% under the 19% in the AV column means that 2% of churches use the GNB on Sundays and AV mid-week. And so on.

5.2 It appears from these figures that, as a generalisation, churches tend to use the same version mid-week and on Sundays, with the exception being that a number which use the AV on Sundays will sometimes use either the NEB or GNB for mid-week Bible study meetings. But this total statistical picture conceals the fact that in particular geographical areas, this tendency to use the GNB as the preferred study version is quite marked (see 2.4e above), and has the effect of making the GNB by far the most popular modern version for this purpose. In overall terms, it is the only version that comes anywhere near to challenging the dominance of the AV.

5.3 It is fair to assume that Bible versions used at midweek meetings reflect the preferences of the more active church attenders. Many of these people will continue to use the AV for basic theological reasons. But the rise in popularity of the GNB at this level must reflect its intelligibility and general usefulness as a study version over against both the AV and other modern translations.

6 Bible Versions, geography and social trends

Is there any relationship between Bible versions and the geography of the Scottish churches?

6.1 Given the dominant use of the AV by the Conservative Presbyterians, we need not be surprised to discover that their main strongholds in the Highlands and Western Isles are wholly committed to the use of this version. The other island communities (Orkney and Shetland), together with other rural areas of the country, are also committed to the AV on the whole, though other versions (especially the GNB) have sufficiently frequent use to feature in the regional statistics.

6.2 In only three areas are modern versions favoured to a sufficiently large degree to become statistically the most popular versions for both Sunday and midweek use across all denominations: in Aberdeen, and in two districts of Strathclyde (Renfrew and Inverclyde; and Eastwood, Bearsden, Milngavie and Strathkelvin). In each of these areas the GNB has become the most popular version of all, for all occasions. In two of these areas, even the Conservative Presbyterians have abandoned their loyalty to the AV and adopted a modern version instead (NIV).

6.3 It is worth noting that these three areas have a high level of social mobility. Aberdeen in particular has seen large population changes in recent years. It is well established that a mobile population tends on the whole to be less likely to attend church. Moving away from familiar surroundings makes it easier to break habits established within close-knit family groups over generations. While the churches in the three areas highlighted here have statistically been neither more nor less successful than churches elsewhere in terms of church growth, the nature of population movements in these districts almost certainly means that they face greater potential difficulties in maintaining attendances.

6.4 We have seen in 4.1-2 above that it is not possible to make a direct statistical link between growing churches and Bible versions – or, at least, not on the kind of statistics produced by this survey. But when other environmental factors are introduced into the equation, there must remain a strong suggestion that the use of the GNB in areas of high mobility can hardly be unrelated to the need for churches to appeal to people who would otherwise be socially disposed to have only minimal (if any) contact with the local churches.

6.5 It could also be argued that the social classes represented most strongly in such mobile populations are more likely to wish to explore the full implications of the gospel both before and after committing themselves to regular church involvement, and for that reason also they are more attracted to use of a Bible version that is both accessible and intelligible.

7 Conclusions

7.1 The Bible has been described as 'the least read bestseller'. For those involved in the promotion of greater Bible use and understanding, the dominance of the AV in the Scottish churches will present a great challenge. Whilst it is true that church growth and individual spirituality cannot be directly assessed in relation to use of particular Bible versions, it is also true that no serious Bible study aids are now based on the AV. Biblical scholars and Christian educators have been agreed for many years that the AV is deficient simply as a translation of the original Biblical languages (quite apart from the question of general intelligibility). Its continuing widespread use reminds us of how far we have yet to go before the results of recent scholarship percolate down from the seminary to the pews (or the pulpit?).

7.2 At the same time, we need to remember that this survey is exclusively concerned with Bible versions used *in church services*. As institutions, the churches in Scotland move notoriously slowly. But it is unlikely that their members follow suit, and those Christians who read and study the Bible regularly in an informal or family context would almost certainly reflect a completely different balance of version preferences.

7.3 The fact that all the versions surveyed here can be linked with churches that are growing, static and declining suggests that church life and Christian commitment are not primarily related to Bible versions. While most churches seem convinced that a modern version is important for full understanding (hence the predominance of the GNB in mid-week study meetings), no one version has a clear claim to mediate the life-giving message of the gospel more than others. Two important conclusions emerge out of this:

7.3a Bible use is of more importance than Bible (version) reading *per se*. It is not what we read, or how we read it, that matters: what we do with it and how we understand it are the crucial elements.

7.3b This simply confirms something we have always known: that real church growth and spiritual vitality comes from the work of the Holy Spirit in the lives of God's people, as the word of God found in Scripture is applied by Him to the circumstances of everyday life in our nation and in each local community.

THE AGE AND SEX OF SCOTTISH CHURCH ATTENDERS COMPARED WITH THE NATIONAL AGE/SEX STRUCTURE

MRS MARY CULLEN

*Chairperson of the
Justice and Peace Commission,
Roman Catholic Church in Scotland*

A general overview of the age and sex of Scottish church attenders shows that people over the age of 65 and under the age of 15 make up a disproportionate number in congregations, compared with their number in the population. 25% of church attenders are under the age of 15, compared with 21% in the civil population, and 22% of church-goers are over the age of 65 although they make up only 14% of the population. There are far fewer people aged 15-19 (5% against 9%), proportionately even fewer aged 20-29 (9% against 15%) and proportionately fewer aged 30-44 (15% against 19%). The percentage of those aged 45-64 is higher than the percentage in the civil population (24% against 22%).

These figures do not show, however, that many more women attend church in all these age groups. 63% of all Scottish church-goers are women, and this percentage is fairly uniform throughout the country.

Boys under the age of 15 who attend church match their proportion in the population, but girls exceed theirs by 4%. Fewer men attend church aged 15-19 (2% against 5%) than women (3% against 4%). In the age group 20-29, the shortfall is made up mostly of men (4%). For those aged 30-44, the difference is entirely with men, as the proportion of women in church exactly matches their proportion in the population. The higher percentage of those aged 45-64 who attend (24% against 22%) conceals the fact that men are deficient by 2% and women more numerous by 4%. Among the oldest, where church attendance is high, women are more numerous than their proportion in the population would suggest (15% against 9%). It is important to note that there is little regional variation on these figures, so that the lack of people, especially males aged 15-44 attending church, poses a very great challenge to all the churches.

Area analysis: variations from the general pattern

Borders
1. The percentage of boys under 15 attending church is 2% less than their percentage in the population. This is low: see also Edinburgh, Orkney, and the Western Isles and Skye and Lochalsh.
2. The percentage of men aged 20-29 is 5% less than the

percentage in the civil population. Compare with Lothian, Renfrew and Inverclyde, and Shetland.
3. The percentage of women aged 45-64 is high (5%), the same as Central and Glasgow.
4. The percentage of those aged 65 and over is 10% more; this is also high.

Central
1. The general pattern is the same as other areas. The percentage of children who attend is 2% more than the percentage in the population, that 2% being female.
2. The percentage of attenders aged 45-64 is 3% less for men, but 5% more for women. This is the highest difference recorded for women in this age group. See also Borders and Glasgow.

Dumfries and Galloway
1. The percentage of boys under 15 attending church is 10% against 11% in the population, a shortfall of 1%. Altogether nine areas show a shortfall for boys.
2. The percentage of men aged 45-64 exactly matches the total percentage in the population (11%). Elsewhere there is a shortfall, except in Western Isles Skye and Lochalsh where there is 1% more.
3. In all other aspects, the figures almost exactly match the national overall figures.

Fife
1. Note that the total percentage of male attenders in all ages is 35% against 49% of the civil population, a shortfall of 14%. The difference is the greatest of all areas, the smallest difference being in the Western Isles, Skye and Lochalsh (6%).
2. The percentage of women aged 15-19 exactly matches the percentage in the population. This is true of only six areas, the others falling below.
3. The percentage of women aged 65 or over is higher than average.

Grampian: Aberdeen
1. The percentage of children under the age of 15 attending church is 3% more than the total percentage in the population, that 3% being female.
2. The percentage of those aged 15-19 is 2% less, an equal shortage of both sexes.

Proportions in each age group	Under 15	15-44	45-64	65 or over
All Scottish church-goers	25%	29%	24%	22%
Male Scottish church-goers	11%	10%	9%	7%
Female Scottish church-goers	14%	19%	15%	15%
Scottish population	21%	43%	22%	14%

3. The percentage of those aged 20-29 is 5% less, 4% male and 1% female.
4. The percentage of men between the ages of 30-44 attending church is higher than average (6% against 5%) but the percentage of women is higher than their percentage in the civil population (10% against 9%).
5. The percentage of both sexes between the ages 15-44 is higher than average (34% against 29%). Compare with Edinburgh and Eastwood, Bearsden & Milngavie and Strathkelvin.

Grampian outside Aberdeen
1. Of the high percentage of children under 15 years attending church (31% against 23%), 18% (out of 31%) are female. This is the highest percentage of girls. Compare with Eastwood, Bearsden and Milngavie, and Strathkelvin.
2. As in Fife and four other areas, the percentage of women aged 15-19 matches that of the civil population. In all other areas it falls below.
3. The percentage of women aged 30-44 falls 1% below the percentage in the population. Compare with Lothian, Orkney and Shetland. All other areas show an increase or match the population percentage.

Highland
1. As in almost half the areas, there is a shortfall between the percentage of boys who attend, and their percentage in the population. As in all other areas, the percentage of girls who attend is higher.
2. As in almost half the areas, the percentage of women aged 30-44 who attend is 1% higher than the percentage in the population. Nowhere has higher than this 1% difference.

Lothian: Edinburgh
1. The percentage of boys under the age of 15 is particularly small – 2% smaller than the percentage in the total population. Compare with Borders and Orkney, and contrast with Eastwood, Bearsden & Milngavie, and Strathkelvin.
2. The percentage of those aged 65 and over is higher than average – 26% against 17%.
3. The percentage of those between the ages of 15 and 44 is higher than average (33% against 29%). See also Aberdeen and Eastwood, Bearsden & Milngavie, Strathkelvin.

Lothian outside Edinburgh
1. Of the high percentage (29% against 23% of the total population) of those under 15 years attending church, 17% are female. Compare Orkney, Shetland and Eastwood, Bearsden & Milngavie and Strathkelvin. There is, however, a large drop in the number of female attenders aged 15-44 (18% against 23%).
2. The percentage of women over 45 who attend is high (29% against 17% in the population).
3. The shortage of manpower in the age range 15-64 is high (17% against 32%).

Orkneys
1. A high percentage of girls under 15 years attend church (17% against 11%). Compare Lothian, Shetland, Grampian and Eastwood, Milngavie & Bearsden and Strathkelvin. In Orkney this is followed by a higher than average drop in female attendance in the age group 15-19 and in 20-44.
2. The percentage of boys attending church is one of the lowest (9% against 11%).

Shetlands
1. Of the high percentage of those under the age of 15 who attend church (30% against 24%) 18% are female. Compare with Grampian.
2. The percentage of men aged 20-29 who attend is 3% against 8%, the highest shortfall. Compare with Borders, Lothian and Renfrew and Inverclyde.
3. Only 17% of church attenders are in the age group 45-64 (overall national figure is 24%).
4. The percentage of women aged 65 and over who attend is high – 17% against 8% in the population. Contrast with the low figure in Eastwood, Bearsden & Milngavie and Strathkelvin.

Strathclyde: Dumbarton, Clydebank, Cumbernauld and Kilsyth
1. The female attendance figures in the 15-19 age group match the percentage for the population of 44%.
2. The shortage of manpower between the ages 15-64 is higher than average (18% attendance against 32% in the population.)
3. The percentage of women over 45 who attend church is higher than average (30% against 18% of the population.) Contrast with Eastwood, Bearsden & Milngavie and Strathkelvin.

Strathclyde: East Kilbride, Hamilton and Lanark
1. The percentage of children under the age of 15 attending church is 6% more than the percentage in the population, the 6% being female. This is a high female percentage.
2. In the age group 15-19 the percentage of women attending matches the percentage in the population of 4%. No area exceeds this percentage difference.
3. There is a smaller than average number of people aged 65 and over who go to church; 17% against 11% of the population, and 22% for churchgoers across the nation.

Strathclyde: Eastwood, Bearsden & Milngavie, and Strathkelvin
1. There is a striking difference in the numbers who attend aged under 15 and over 45. The percentage of boys attending church is 3% more than the percentage in the population, and this is the highest percentage of all areas. The percentage of girls attending is also high (17% against 11%).
2. A high proportion of adults aged 15-44 attend church (35%) but the percentage of women only matches that of the population – every other area shows a percentage increase.
3. The percentage of attenders over the age of 65 is small (only 1% more than the percentage in the population.) This is the lowest percentage increase. Compare with Dumbarton, Clydebank, Cumbernauld and Kilsyth.

Strathclyde: Glasgow
1. Of those aged under 15 years who attend church, the male percentage matches that of the population of 10%, the female attendance is 13% against 10%.
2. A high percentage of church attenders above the age of 45 are women (34% against 22% in the population.) Compare with Borders.

Strathclyde: Kyle and Carrick, Cunnock and Doun Valley, Kilmarnock and Loudoun, and Cunninghame
1. The percentage of boys under 15 who attend is greater

than their percentage in the population (12% against 11%). Only two other areas show the same percentage difference; see Grampian outside Aberdeen, and Eastwood, Bearsden & Milngavie and Strathkelvin.
2. As in five other areas, the percentage of women aged 15-19 matches the population percentage. In all other areas it falls below.

Strathclyde: Renfrew and Inverclyde
1. Of those under the age of 15 who attend church, the male percentage of 11% matches the percentage in the population. The female difference of 2% is the most common, though lowest, of all.
2. The percentage of men in the age group 20-29 is particularly low (3% against 8%). Compare Borders, Lothian and Shetland.

Strathclyde: Motherwell and Monklands
1. The general pattern is the same as other areas, with a shortfall of boys aged under 15, and a consistent shortage of manpower between the ages 15-64 (20% against 34%). Compare this with female church attendance in the same age group of 34% against 33%.

Tayside: Dundee
1. The general pattern is the same as other areas, the percentage of children under 15 who attend being 2% more
2. The percentage of those aged 65 and over is 9% more, 7% of whom are women. This is slightly higher than average.

Tayside: Other
1. Of those under the age of 15 who attend church, the male percentage of 10% matches that of the population, the female attendance is 12% against 10%.
2. The percentage of women aged 20-29 attending church is the same as the percentage in the civil population. Everywhere else records a shortfall of between 1% and 3%.

Western Isles, Skye and Lochalsh
1. The percentage of boys under the age of 15 attending church is 2% less than the percentage in the population (10% against 12%), the percentage of girls 2% more (13% against 11%).
2. Note that the general pattern of a large drop in male attendance between the years 15 and 44 is not so marked here, where male attendance remains closer to the percentage of males in the total population.
3. The percentage of men aged 45-64 is higher than the male percentage for this age group in the population – 11% against 10%. This is the only area where this is so.
4. The general pattern of female attendance is close to the overall pattern.

Denominational Analysis
An examination of the figures by denomination show the same overall pattern, but with more variation. More Roman Catholics attend church in Scotland than any other single group – 287,000 adults or 7% of the adult population. Next comes the Church of Scotland with 266,000 adults, 7% of the adult population. The remaining 3% of church-going adults come from the Independent churches – 27,000; the Conservative Presbyterians – 17,000; the Scottish Episcopal Church – 16,000; the Baptists – 21,000 and the Other denominations – 26,000.

Baptist congregations have by far the highest percentage of attenders in the 15-44 age group (this almost matches the percentage in the total population of 43%.) Baptists do not show the same age gap as other congregations: children, parents and grandchildren attend church. The Conservative Presbyterians have the smallest percentage of children, and the largest proportion of over 65's they are also the denomination in fastest decline. This pattern of large numbers of old people and a small number of children is serious, as is the drop in attendance between the ages of 15 and 44 which is marked in all denominations. The Church of Scotland and the Baptist Church have a higher than average number of children attending, and Independent and Catholic children attend in high numbers.

Church of Scotland
1. The percentage of children under the age of 15 is 3% more than the total percentage of children in the population.
2. The percentage of those aged 15-44 is 14% less than the total percentage in the population. This is higher than the average for all the denominations.
3. The percentage of those aged 45-64 is 3% more than the total civil percentage.
4. The percentage of attenders over the age of 65 is 8% more than the total civil percentage.

Conservative Presbyterians
1. The percentage of those under the age of 15 is smallest of all the denominations, and represents a decline over 4 years of 8%.
2. The percentage of those aged 65 and over is higher than average.

Scottish Episcopal
1. This is the fastest growing denomination (23% more child attenders and 9% adult attenders over 4 years).
2. It has the smallest proportion of children (2% less than the proportion in the population.)
3. There is a lower than average proportion of people aged 15-44, and a higher than average proportion of those aged 65 and over.

Baptist
1. The percentage of those aged 15-44 is the highest proportion of all denominations.

Denomination/age group summary	Under 15	15-44	45-64	65 or over
Church of Scotland	24%	29%	25%	22%
Conservative Presbyterian	19%	31%	24%	26%
Scottish Episcopal	19%	33%	25%	23%
Baptist	24%	41%	18%	17%
Independent	28%	32%	19%	21%
Other Denominations	26%	32%	20%	22%
Scottish population	21%	43%	22%	14%

Independent
1. The percentage of those under the age of 15 is above average.
2. The percentage of those aged 15-44 is also above the average for all Protestant churches, but the percentage of those aged 45-64 is smaller than average.

Roman Catholic
The attendance in age groups shows little difference from the Protestant proportions, except that there are more Catholic children and teenagers going to church which may be due to the strength of Catholic schools, but there is a similar drop in attendance after the age of 19 as with Protestant churches.

Nearly half of the Catholics who go to church on Sundays are over 45. Roman Catholic men attend in greater numbers than Protestants – average of 42% against overall male church attendance of 37%; but this falls short of the proportion of males in the population (48%).

Child attendance by area and denomination
Of all those going to church in Scotland in 1984, 203,000 were children against 209,000 in 1980. This is a drop of 3%, but it should be seen against an 8% drop in the overall child population. Scottish churches therefore held on to their child attenders more successfully than their adult members.

The churches with an increase in child attendance were Scottish Episcopal (23%) and Other Denominations (2%). Those with greatest losses were Conservative Presbyterians (8%) and Independents (7%). Roman Catholic loss was 3%, the same as the Church of Scotland, and the Baptist loss was 2%.

The figures also vary by area as the table shows.

The Church of Scotland had a significant child attendance growth in 10 areas, against an overall decrease of 3%. Shetland had the highest growth (26%) with Strathclyde: East Kilbride, Hamilton and Lanark at 15%. The greatest fall was in Glasgow.

The Conservative Presbyterians saw great losses in child attendance, and numbers in all areas are small. Both the large percentage growth in Aberdeen (33%) and the loss of 19% in the Western Isles, Skye and Lochalsh are based on particularly small numbers.

The Scottish Episcopal Church shows a child attendance decrease in only one area; Eastwood, Bearsden & Milngavie and Strathkelvin. Elsewhere the growth is very striking, particularly in Grampian which is based on greater numbers than Aberdeen. All numbers, however, are relatively small.

Baptist child attendance is in decline more than the average in many areas, particularly in Fife and Glasgow. There is a large growth in child attendance in rural Highland.

The increase in child attendance among the Independent churches is particularly marked in Grampian, Borders and Tayside, while the greatest decline is in the urban areas of Strathclyde and Central.

The Other churches are small in number, and the large percentage decrease in child attendance in Dumfries and Galloway (25%) is based on particularly small numbers. The greatest growth is in Fife.

Roman Catholic child attendance increase is most marked in Borders and Eastwood, Bearsden & Milngavie and Strathkelvin. Compare with the loss in Fife and Tayside.

	Church of Scotland	Conservative Presbyterian	Scottish Episcopal	Baptist	Independent	Other	Roman Catholic
Borders	+6%	–	+10%	–13%	+29%	+14%	+15%
Central	+10%	0%	+41%	+7%	–16%	+7%	+2%
Dumfries & Galloway	–11%	0%	+17%	+18%	–4%	–25%	–8%
Fife	+4%	†	+21%	–23%	+13%	+32%	–9%
Grampian: Aberdeen	–19%	+33%	+50%	+17%	+24%	–11%	–8%
Grampian: Other	+2%	0%	+54%	+23%	–8%	–7%	+6%
Glasgow: Renfrew etc.	–9%	0%	+46%	–12%	–2%	+7%	–3%
Highland	+9%	+13%	+21%	+46%	–6%	–8%	+3%
Lothian: Edinburgh	–10%	0%	+8%	–5%	–13%	–13%	–15%
Lothian: Other	–9%	†	+23%	+9%	+4%	+9%	+14%
Orkneys	–14%	–	0%	–13%	0%	0%	0%
Shetlands	+26%	–	0%	+23%	+4%	–9%	0%
Strathclyde: Dumbarton etc	+5%	0%	+10%	–10%	–8%	+18%	+7%
Strathclyde: East Kilbride etc	+15%	0%	+40%	–10%	–18%	–4%	0%
Strathclyde : Kyle & Carrick etc	+8%	0%	+32%	+13%	–9%	+16%	–5%
Strathclyde: Eastwood etc	+2%	0%	–8%	–13%	–21%	–11%	+15%
Strathclyde: Glasgow	–21%	–8%	+25%	–16%	–13%	+13%	–5%
Strathclyde: Motherwell etc.	–4%	†	+33%	–6%	–12%	–18%	–5%
Tayside: Dundee	–1%	†	+10%	–10%	+7%	–15%	–5%
Tayside: Other	–12%	†	+33%	+24%	+25%	+3%	–10%
Western Isles etc.	–8%	–19%	0%	–	0%	0%	+9%
OVERALL	–3%	–8%	+23%	–2%	–7%	+2%	–3%

† Numbers too small to give a meaningful percentage.

Urban children tend to go to church less, although Aberdeen had the same percentage as average (29%). Rural areas saw a higher than average attendance, with Grampian 41% of the adult population and Orkney 38%.

On average well over 90% of children who go to church on Sunday also attend Sunday School. (This does not apply to Catholic children.) It is interesting that the Scottish Episcopal Church has the fastest growing number of children but the smallest proportion in Sunday school (91%).

Comments and questions

Information of the kind contained in this report gives rise to many challenging and important questions for the church regarding its vitality, its image and its leadership, and ultimately its effectiveness in preaching the Word of God to all people. The particular aspect of the report dealt with in this essay shows that Church attenders overall in Scotland are out of proportion to the population. The church has a preponderance of women, children and the elderly. Since only 17% of the entire Scottish population attends church, the greatest problem facing the church must be the large numbers of people who fail to see any relevance in church attendance, particularly the number of young and active men whom it fails to engage.

Are women more faithful to the church or less critical than the men who leave? Is it not an anomaly that churches that are made up of so many women are led by men? On the evidence shown in this report, it would appear that many adults who do not attend church send their children, but feel it has little to do with the business of their own everyday living.

Questions for the churches might be:

1. Does my church involve itself in the community and in community problems (housing, unemployment etc) or is its agenda ecclesiastical and inward looking?
2. Is it concerned with the needs and aspirations of young people?
3. Is its worship flexible in style and content?
4. Does it encourage its lay people to take an active and creative part in building up the church community?

Information gathered here, although it is of great interest to the church and should prompt much reflection, is in the end based on a head count, and says little about the quality of the body of the church and the relationships within it. It does not indicate the strength of the renewal movements within and across denominations – the prayer groups, house groups, peace and justice groups and the ecumenical movement. The church is also affected by movements in society.

The relative strength of child and teenage attendance in Catholic churches suggests a strong link with systematic religious education in schools. The drop in attendance in all the denominations in the age group immediately afterwards may suggest the need for some kind of adult education in the faith.

An area of research might be to discover the correlation of church attendance and social deprivation, so that the churches might see precisely where they are or are not present to those with whom Jesus concerned himself: the poor and the weak of society.

METHODOLOGY, NOTES & DEFINITIONS

PETER BRIERLEY
European Director,
MARC Europe

Introduction

In November 1979 a census of the churches in England was undertaken by the British and Foreign Bible Society under the auspices of the Nationwide Initiative in Evangelism. The subsequent report *Prospects for the Eighties* gave up-to-date information on church membership and attendance, both by denomination and county. Seeing the usefulness of such a compendium of data the National Bible Society of Scotland (NBSS) and MARC Europe ageed to undertake a similar census for the churches in Scotland. The personnel in MARC at that time had just completed a similar service for Welsh churches and the report *Prospects for Wales* was published in 1983.

Building on the experience gained through the English and Welsh studies a questionnaire was drawn up and piloted during late 1983. A copy of the final version used for the Church of Scotland is reproduced on the page after next; this was sent (with wording slightly changed for each denomination as appropriate) to all churches in Scotland for completion for the month of March 1984. Church of Scotland forms were sent to Session Clerks.

Response

There were an estimated 4,063 churches at the time of the census, and information was received from 3,029 of these, an overall response rate of 74.7%. The actual rate naturally varied from one part of Scotland to another, and from one denomination to another. The individual response rates for each are shown at the head of the statistical pages in this Report. This is an excellent response rate, and reflects the level of concern among local church leaders over the situation in Scotland.

About 45% of the churches responded initially, and a further 15% when sent a reminder. Details from 15% more were obtained by telephoning those who at that stage had not replied – a mammoth task willingly undertaken by a small team organised through Fergus Macdonald, General Secretary of the NBSS.

Details collected

Church Adherents Collected for 1980 and 1984. The definition of adherent varies from one denomination to another. The number of adherents has been added to the number of church members for the Free Church of Scotland and the Free Presbyterian Church of Scotland throughout, as their definition of adherent is closer to other churches' definitions of membership, thus allowing more consistent comparisons.

Church Membership Collected for 1980 and 1984. The definition of membership varies from one denomination to another. The Roman Catholic Church estimates of their population include children.

Church Attendance Collected as the "average on Sundays in March" in 1980 and 1984. Adult (those aged 15 years and over) and Sunday School attendance were requested separately, as was the number of individual adults who attended *both* morning and evening (where two services were held). This latter figure of "twicers" was not always given. Where churches holding two services did not state a figure, it was assumed that the proportion would be the same as for those churches which did give details, for that area and denomination. Afternoon services were counted as evening services for the purposes of this study.

Where the Report gives figures of church *attenders*, this refers to individuals attending at least one service morning or evening, that is, "twicers" are excluded. If information on total church *attendance* is required, counting those going twice two times, then the figures given need to be increased by the percentage of "twicers" indicated (13% for the whole of Scotland).

Some churches were unable to give a 1980 attendance figure; it was assumed that the 1980 attendance would be as for other churches (who gave both figures) in that area for that denomination. The 1980 figures were confirmed by denominational data where obtainable except in the case of the Conservative Presbyterians. This, together with the relatively small number of Free Presbyterian congregations returning a 1980 figure has to be borne in mind in interpreting the Conservative Presbyterians' rate of decline.

Roman Catholic figures were taken from their returns for November 1981 and 1983. These were taken unchanged as proxy for March 1982 and 1984 respectively, and the change between these two years was then extrapolated to give estimated March 1980 figures. These figures include a proportion of children under the age of 15, and from an estimate of this proportion given by Right Rev Joseph Devine, Bishop of Motherwell, the adult figures were derived.

Some Conservative Presbyterian churches in the urban areas included children aged 7-15 in their attendance figures for 1980 as they attended the first part of morning service before leaving for Sunday School. Estimates of these were subtracted, based on the civil population proportions.

The Methodist Church, through Richard Smith, were able to supply from their administrative records, details of membership and attendance of all their churches. Those

Methodist churches not responding had their November 1979 and 1983 figures taken as proxy for March 1980 and 1984 respectively.

Age of Attenders These were collected for 1984 Protestant congregations only. This question was less well answered, but the degree of response, both by denomination and county, is indicated in the Report, expressed as a percentage of all Protestant churches in Scotland. Overall 66% of the churches were able to give this information, representing seven-eighths of all the responding churches.

Not every church has a Sunday School, and not every child going to church attends a Sunday School even if there is one. Details of the latter were obtained by comparing the number of children under 15 attending the church and the number going to Sunday School. Sometimes the numbers of young people associated with a church bore little resemblance to adult membership.

No age distribution of church-goers was included on Roman Catholic forms, as many of their churches have very large numbers attending, and to attempt to assess the age breakdown would have been very difficult. Instead estimates were made by observers counting congregations at all services of a few churches (4% in total). Those chosen depended on where volunteers worshipped, and so are not random, but their figures are the only indication available of the proportions.

Number of Ministers These were obtained from the number of churches for which each individual was responsible. The total per denomination was already known from the denominational headquarters. Some ministers, especially in rural areas, look after several churches.

Midweek Meetings Churches were asked to indicate whether, apart from their Sunday services, they held meetings of any form where the Bible was studied. 59% held one or more meeting of this type. Details of the nature of the meeting were not requested, but the number attending was given. So also was the version of the Bible normally used.

Bible Version The version(s) of the Bible normally used on a Sunday for public reading in church was requested. The following abbreviations have been used throughout this Report:

AV = Authorised Version (King James Version)
GNB = Good News Bible
NEB = New English Bible
RSV = Revised Standard Version
NIV = New International Version
JER = Jerusalem Bible

Civil Population The adult and child figures have been taken from the 1981 census figures published by the Office of Population Censuses and Surveys (OPCS). The rate of change of both adult and child population is measured between the censuses of 1971 and 1981, as published by OPCS, and extrapolated to give a four year figure.

Analysis

The data thus collected was computerised. The totals for each statistic were grossed up according to the response rate for each denomination and area. The membership totals were then compared with the published Protestant denominational totals, and found on average to be 2% higher reflecting a tendency for the forms to be returned by the larger churches. The grossed figures were therefore reduced by the appropriate denominational percentage, which was also applied to the number of attenders, so that the ratio of attenders to members remained the same. A few other adjustments were made to the data, usually when only partial details were given in certain denominational/ area groupings which had just a small number of churches; the direction of trend was however always maintained. All figures have been rounded to the nearest 10.

The size of Scottish churches was counted on a finer grid than is given in this Report – in groups of five up to 25, then in 25's up to 150, 50's up to 400, and so on. These more detailed percentages may be obtained from MARC Europe. The averages, or means, were based on these narrower groupings, giving a more accurate figure.

Growing churches were defined as those whose attendance had increased by at least 20% over the four years 1980-1984 for churches with 1984 attenders numbering 50 or more, or an increase of at least 100% for churches with fewer than 50 attenders in 1984. These criteria are fairly rigorous, partly to conform with the English and Welsh church growth data already published, and partly to ensure that any growth thus recorded was real. Thus a church with 10 attenders in 1980 which grew to 12 in 1984 (a 20% increase) would not be counted as a growing church; but if its 1984 number was 20 or more (a 100% increase) it would have been. A church with 60 attenders in 1980 would be counted as a growing church if its numbers in 1984 were 72 or more (a 20% increase).

Rates of change for attenders and members have been calculated over the four year period based on 1980.

Denominations

After the analysis of the returns had been completed, the *Church of Scotland* published their official communicant membership figure for end-1983 of 902,714. This compares with the Census figure of 907,920 (½% higher, and within the estimated margins). The reflection of this official figure by area came too late to be carried through; the essayists also have made their comments based on the higher figure.

Conservative Presbyterian churches include 210 Free Church of Scotland churches and preaching centres, 77 Free Presbyterian Church of Scotland churches, and 5 Reformed Presbyterian Church of Scotland churches.

Baptist churches include those of the Baptist Union of Scotland, 8 independent Baptist churches, 4 Grace Baptist, and an estimated 12 independent Baptist churches of the Reformed tradition.

Independent churches include those belonging to the Christian Brethren, open and closed, 18 in the Fellowship of Independent Evangelical Churches, an estimated 30 House Churches, and 99 churches in the Congregational Union.

The *Other Denominations* is a composite group of churches brought together because no one entity within them is large enough to justify separate statistical tabulation and percentage calculations when disaggregated by county. The group consists of Methodist churches (73); the United Free Church of Scotland (83), United Reformed Church (8), and the Fellowship of Churches of Christ (3); the Salvation Army (126 corps); the Apostolic church (27), the Assemblies of God (17), the Church of the Nazarene (19) and the Elim Pentecostal Church (19); the Religious Society of Friends (20), Seventh Day Adventists (10), Ecumenical Experiment churches (5), City Missions or Gospel Halls (12), German (3), Polish (2), Lutheran (2), Church of God (2), Church of God of Prophecy (1), other independent churches (10), and churches of the Orthodox tradition (3).

The *Roman Catholic* figures include one Liberal Catholic, and one Ukrainian Catholic church.

CENSUS OF CHURCH ATTENDANCE IN SCOTLAND

The purpose of this census is to gather information which will provide a national picture of Church attendance and activities. This will give Churches and other organisations facts which will help them to appraise the effectiveness of their mission, and to plan for more effective action.

PLEASE USE BLOCK CAPITALS

1. Minister: 2. Session Clerk

    Name: _____   Name: _____

    Address: _____   _____

    _____   _____

    Post Code: _____   Post Code: _____

3. Church

    Name: _____   City/Town/Village _____

4. Other Churches

4a Is the Minister named in (1) above responsible for churches other than that named in (3) above? YES/NO*
4b If 'Yes', please give the name and town/village in which those churches are located.

    _____   _____

    _____   _____

5. Church Membership	1984	1980
a) Number of Church Members for church named in (3) above	____	____
b) Number of Adult adherents for church named in (3) above	____	____

6. Average Church Attendance on Sundays in March for church named in (3) above (i.e. total attendance over the 4 Sundays divided by 4)

	1984	1980
a) Total adult attendance (aged 15 and over) at morning service(s)	____	____
b) Total adult attendance (aged 15 and over) at afternoon and evening service(s)	____	____
c) Please try to estimate how many adults attended both services (i.e. came twice) – where two are held – on an average Sunday in March.	____	____
d) Children (aged under 15) attending Sunday School, BB Class, etc., on an average Sunday in March	____	

e) We appreciate it is difficult, but it would be a great help if you could please estimate the approximate numbers, by sex and age group, of those attending Church, Sunday School, etc., on an average Sunday in March.

	Male	Female
Under 15 years	____	____
15-19 years	____	____
20-29 years	____	____
30-44 years	____	____
45-64 years	____	____
65 and over	____	____

7. What is the regular language of worship in your church? English/Gaelic/Both*

8. Which version(s) of the Bible is most often read publicly in church?

    [ ] A.V.   [ ] G.N.B.   [ ] Jerusalem   [ ] Other
    [ ] N.E.B. [ ] N.I.V.   [ ] R.S.V.

9. Bible Use

9a Apart from Sunday services, does the Church named in (3) above have any form of service/meeting/group to study the Bible?   YES/NO*

9b If 'Yes', how many on average attend?   _____

9c Which version of the Bible is normally used?   _____

10. NAME OF RESPONDENT _____   Date _____

Please send the completed form to Rev. Fergus Macdonald, N.B.S.S., 7 Hampton Terrace, Edinburgh, EH12 5XU.

Thank you for your help.   *Please delete as appropriate

CHURCH OF SCOTLAND

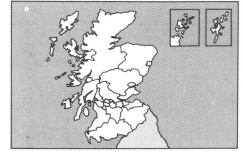

Total Adult Population:	3,957,410
Change of adult population in four years:	+1%
Total number of Church of Scotland Churches 1984:	1,790
Percentage of Churches responding:	82%
Total number of Church of Scotland ministers:	1,451
Percentage of Church of Scotland churches holding mid-week meetings:	53%
Percentage mid-week attendance of Sunday attendance:	6%
1984 adult Church of Scotland church membership as percentage of total adult population:	23%
1984 adult Church of Scotland church attenders as percentage of total adult population:	6.7%
1984 adult Church of Scotland adherents as percentage of total adult population:	1.2%

	Child Attenders 1980	Child Attenders **1984**	Change %	Children under 15 attending Sunday school 1984 %	Adult Attenders 1980	Adult Attenders **1984**	Change %	Adults who attended twice on Sunday 1984 %	Membership 1980	Membership **1984**	Change %
Total all churches	209,150	**203,260**	−3	97	677,920	**660,360**	−3	13	1,929,900	**1,876,840**	−3
Church of Scotland	98,360	**95,040**	−3	97	272,660	**266,300**	−2	11	953,940	**907,920**	−5
Percentage Church of Scotland is of total:	47%	**47%**			40%	**40%**			50%	**49%**	

	Percentage of churches which between 1980 & 1984: Grew %	Remained Static %	Declined %	1984 Churches whose services are in: Gaelic only %	Gaelic & English %	English only %	1984 Churches whose services are in the: Morning only %	Morn. & Evening %	Evening only %
All Churches	26	52	22	½	1½	98	43	53	4
Church of Scotland	29	41	30	0	2	98	59	40	1
Version of Bible most used on Sunday	NEB	AV	AV						

	All Church Attenders[1] Male %	Female %	Total %	All Scottish Protestant Churches Male %	Female %	Total %
Age Group						
Under 15	11	13	24	11	14	25
15-19	2	3	5	2	3	5
20-29	3	6	9	3	6	9
30-44	5	10	15	5	10	15
45-64	9	16	25	9	15	24
65 or over	7	15	22	7	15	22
All ages	37	63	100	37	63	100

Number Attending Church per week excluding twicers	Church of Scotland Churches[2] Growing %	Static %	Declining %	All churches %	All Scottish Protestant Churches Growing %	Static %	Declining %	All churches %
Under 10	0	0	1	0	2	5	4	4
10-25	1	7	17	9	4	17	18	14
26-50	2	17	23	15	6	26	22	19
51-100	11	19	34	21	22	19	35	23
101-150	14	19	16	17	15	13	13	13
151-200	18	15	7	14	14	9	6	10
201-300	27	16	2	15	19	8	2	10
Over 300	27	7	0	9	18	3	0	7
TOTAL	100	100	100	100	100	100	100	100
Average Sunday congregation (No. of adults morning and evening)	234	139	74	149	182	90	69	108

[1]This table is based on responses from 71% of all Church of Scotland churches
[2]This table is based on responses from 81% of all Church of Scotland churches

THE CHURCH OF SCOTLAND

Rev Dr I B DOYLE
*Secretary, Church of
Scotland Department of
Ministry and Mission*

This survey will underline concern about falling membership rolls within the Church of Scotland, but there are certain features which modify anxiety and indeed make hopeful pointers to the future.

It has to be acknowledged on the one hand that membership within the Church of Scotland continues to decline, in the past four years by 5%; but on the other hand, it is worthy of note that church attendance within the same period has declined by only 2%. In other words, the decline would seem to be more marked among nominal members.

Similarly, while the child population of Scotland has dropped over these four years by 8%, child attendance at church has declined by only 3%. Perhaps then it is true to say that the decline in membership may be suggesting a smaller but more committed membership, a better base for the task of mission which this survey undoubtedly reveals.

The survey confirms common feeling that there is an imbalance of sexes and even more of age groups within the Church. People between the ages of 20 and 44 are seriously under-represented. The only age group where the proportion of church attenders is greater than the same proportion of civil population is in the age group 45 to 64. Somehow we have to recruit men and young people into the Church.

Certain areas of the country show encouraging trends. The Borders Region, and Dumfries and Galloway show definite increases of attendance, of 5% and 8%

respectively. Orkney shows an increase of 3% in attendance, while its northern neighbour, Shetland, has to confess to a fall of 10%. These are more difficult statistics to explain than those of Grampian, where the rise of 1% in membership and 2% in attendance is clearly the result of new workers moving into the area. The cities, with the exception of Dundee, show real problems. Aberdeen with a decrease in membership of 3%, reveals a decrease of 11% in church attendance. Edinburgh, with a decrease in membership of 7% shows an almost similar decrease of 6% in attendance. Glasgow, with an adult population decrease of 7%, shows a decrease of 11% in membership and 12% in attendance. Dundee of the four cities, with a drop of 1% in population, has a decrease in membership of 3% but an increase of 7% in attendance. It may well be that the housing areas of our cities where so many people live are still too largely untouched by the Church.

Certain of these statistics may seem obvious to readers. Some leave us wondering why. But two things are made abundantly clear. Firstly, there is a great field of mission for the Church. If for our comfort we quote that 17% of the entire Scottish population attend church regularly, then 83% do not! This represents the staggering total of about four million people; a vast area of concern for all who call themselves Christian.

On the other hand, it is still true that every Sunday something like 660,000 adults go to church. Of these 266,000 go to Church of Scotland congregations. Add to that the fact that still in this past year over 200,000 children attended church, of whom nearly 100,000 are Church of Scotland. With the strength of the Roman Catholic Church added to that of the smaller denominations, 47%, about half of Scotland's adult population, are members of the Christian Church. This is and should be seen as a great base for mission. The slowing down of the fall in church attendance, which the Survey seems to reveal, with the up-turn visible in some areas, may herald a new opportunity. The Church of Scotland, with its nationwide network of people and buildings, with its major share in the Christian population of Scotland, must seek such renewal of its life and worship and witness as will commend effectively the Gospel of Christ.

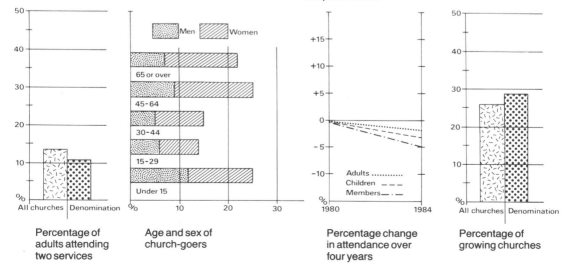

Percentage of
adults attending
two services

Age and sex of
church-goers

Percentage change
in attendance over
four years

Percentage of
growing churches

CONSERVATIVE PRESBYTERIAN CHURCHES

Total Adult Population:	3,957,410
Change of adult population in four years:	+1%
Total number of Conservative Presbyterian churches 1984:	292
Percentage of Churches responding:	69%
Total number of Conservative Presbyterian ministers:	118
Percentage of Conservative Presbyterian churches holding mid-week meetings:	64%
Percentage mid-week attendance of Sunday attendance:	20%
1984 adult Conservative Presbyterian church membership[3] as percentage of total adult population:	0.6% [4]
1984 adult Conservative Presbyterian church attenders as percentage of total adult population:	0.4%

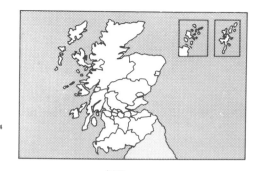

	Child Attenders			Children under 15 attending Sunday school	Adult Attenders			Adults who attended twice on Sunday	Membership		
	1980	**1984**	Change	1984	1980	**1984**	Change	1984	1980	**1984**	Change
			%	%			**%**	%	%			%
Total all churches	209,150	**203,260**	− 3	97	677,920	**660,360**	− 3	13	1,929,900	**1,876,840**	− 3
Conservative Presbyterian	4,280	**3,920**	− 8	93	18,930	**17,130**	− 10	51	27,550	**25,180**	− 9
Percentage Conservative Presbyterian churches are of total:	2%	**2%**			3%	**3%**			1%	**1%**	

	Percentage of churches which between 1980 & 1984:			1984 Churches whose services are in:			1984 Churches whose services are in the:		
	Grew	Remained Static	Declined	Gaelic only	Gaelic & English	English only	Morning only	Morn. & Evening	Evening only
	%	%	%	%	%	%	%	%	%
All Churches	26	52	22	½	1½	98	43	53	4
Conservative Presbyterian	14	72	14	4	14	82	12	72	16
Version of Bible most used on Sunday	AV	AV	AV						

	All Church Attenders[1]			All Scottish Protestant Churches		
	Male	Female	Total	Male	Female	Total
	%	%	%	%	%	%
Under 15	9	10	19	11	14	25
15-19	3	4	7	2	3	5
20-29	4	5	9	3	6	9
30-44	7	8	15	5	10	15
45-64	10	14	24	9	15	24
65 or over	10	16	26	7	15	22
All ages	43	57	100	37	63	100

Number Attending Church per week excluding twicers	Conservative Presbyterian Churches[2]				All Scottish Protestant Churches			
	Growing	Static	Declining	All churches	Growing	Static	Declining	All churches
	%	%	%	%	%	%	%	%
Under 10	11	14	15	14	2	5	4	4
10-25	11	35	26	30	4	17	18	14
26-50	4	29	33	26	6	26	22	19
51-100	38	12	18	17	22	19	35	23
101-150	15	3	0	4	15	13	13	13
151-200	7	4	4	4	14	9	6	10
201-300	7	1	4	3	19	8	2	10
Over 300	7	2	0	2	18	3	0	7
TOTAL	100	100	100	100	100	100	100	100
Average Sunday congregation (No. of adults morning & evening)	108	46	47	59	182	90	69	108

[1] This table is based on responses from 55% of all Conservative Presbyterian churches
[2] This table is based on responses from 66% of all Conservative Presbyterian churches
[3] Including adherents
[4] Of which members 0.3% and adherents 0.3%

CONSERVATIVE PRESBYTERIAN CHURCHES

Dr NEIL MACKAY
Formerly British Council Representative in Argentina

Restricted numbers and the "Presbyterian" label explain this slot in the census. "Conservative" signifies, essentially, a staunch adherence to the doctrine of the plenary inspiration of Scripture, and to the Westminster Confession of Faith as the subordinate standard.

Territorially, there is less overlap. In Scotland, the Reformed Presbyterian Church is confined to a few congregations in the Lowlands. The Free Church of Scotland and the Free Presbyterian Church are at their strongest in the Highlands and Islands (excluding the Orkneys and Shetlands). Because of this preponderance, and without disrespect to congregations elsewhere, I shall confine my comment to the two areas of greatest statistical significance in the schedules: (i) The Western Isles with Skye and Lochalsh, and (ii) The Highlands excluding (i) but including Argyll and Bute.

It is difficult to correlate the raw data of the census with statistical information otherwise available about the strengths, absolute and relative, of the two Churches within the prescribed areas. Various factors can be thought of as contributing to observed discrepancies: for example, the notorious difficulty in defining the word "adherent"; and the problem of estimating church attendances during a communion season (e.g. February to April) in Lewis, when there is a constant swirl of outside attendance from one church to another at successive weekends. Gone, alas, are the days (which I can remember) when Sabbath communion services were held in the open air because of the crowds assembling from other congregations, far and near.

Decline is not limited to such special occasions. Whichever set of statistics we peruse, we find depressingly familiar decreases in numbers in almost all the categories under review. (I say "almost all" because in one or two, particularly in church attendance in the Western Isles, Free Church statistics show a slower rate of decline than this census). The underlying causes are to be found, not so much in a lessening of genuine interest in religion as in trends in the general population of the two areas we are considering.

The total population of the Highlands and Islands reached a maximum in the Disruption decade, and then declined – very rapidly in some cases. It stabilised in the 1960s, and since then has shown a constant growth which has to be related to development of the North Sea oil industry. The one big exception to these general trends was the island of Lewis and Harris, where the population continued to increase until 1911; thereafter there was a steep decline until fairly recently, and now there is an upturn. The picture is one of Southward migration and overseas emigration caused by economic insufficiency. The outgoing tide left behind a large number of fragile communities and, in the Western Isles, a population with an elderly group, especially females, well above the national average. These weaknesses and anomalies have been reflected in the structure of the church population, and the resulting decrease in the under-16 age group must cause great concern. The impact of oil-related industries, both quantitatively (influx and internal migration) and qualitatively (influence on life and tradition) cannot yet be assessed, but experience in similar communities in other parts of the world leaves no great room for optimism.

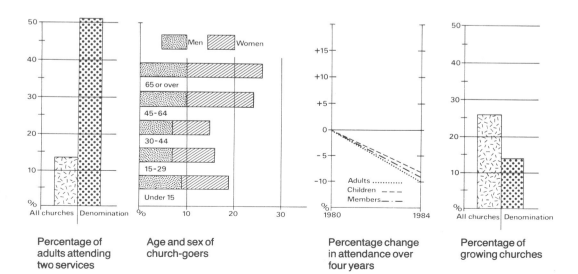

Percentage of adults attending two services

Age and sex of church-goers

Percentage change in attendance over four years

Percentage of growing churches

SCOTTISH EPISCOPAL CHURCH

Total Adult Population:	3,957,410
Change of adult population in four years:	+1%
Total number of Episcopal churches 1984:	306
Percentage of Churches responding:	59%
Total number of Episcopal ministers:	235
Percentage of Episcopal churches holding mid-week meetings:	54%
Percentage mid-week attendance of Sunday attendance:	12%
1984 adult Episcopal church membership as percentage of total adult population:	1.0%
1984 adult Episcopal church attenders as percentage of total adult population:	0.4%
1984 adult Episcopal church adherents as percentage of total adult population:	0.4%

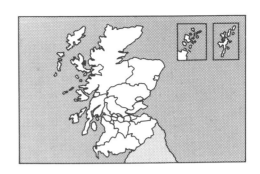

	Child Attenders			Children under 15 attending Sunday school	Adult Attenders			Adults who attended twice on Sunday	Membership		
	1980	**1984**	Change	1984	1980	**1984**	Change	1984	1980	**1984**	Change
			%	%		**%**	%	%			%
Total all churches	209,150	**203,260**	−3	97	677,920	**660,360**	−3	13	1,929,900	**1,876,840**	−3
Episcopal	3,390	**4,170**	+23	91	14,530	**15,830**	+9	11	40,960	**39,610**	−3
Percentage Episcopal Church is of total:	2%	**2%**			2%	**2%**			2%	**2%**	

	Percentage of churches which between 1980 & 1984:			1984 Churches whose services are in:			1984 Churches whose services are in the:		
	Grew	Remained Static	Declined	Gaelic only	Gaelic & English	English only	Morning only	Morn. & Evening	Evening only
	%	%	%	%	%	%	%	%	%
All Churches	26	52	22	½	1½	98	43	53	4
Scottish Episcopal Church	27	65	8	0	1	99	59	38	3
Version of Bible most used on Sunday	NEB	AV	AV/NEB						

	All Church Attenders[1]			All Scottish Protestant Churches		
Age Group	Male	Female	Total	Male	Female	Total
	%	%	%	%	%	%
Under 15	9	10	19	11	14	25
15-19	2	4	6	2	3	5
20-29	4	4	8	3	6	5
30-44	7	12	19	5	10	15
45-64	9	16	25	9	15	24
65 or over	7	16	23	7	15	22
All ages	38	62	100	37	63	100

	Scottish Episcopal Church[2]				All Scottish Protestant Churches			
Number Attending Church per week excluding twicers	Growing	Static	Declining	All churches	Growing	Static	Declining	All churches
	%	%	%	%	%	%	%	%
Under 10	0	10	16	8	2	5	4	4
10-25	12	25	38	22	4	17	18	14
26-50	6	39	0	27	6	26	22	19
51-100	47	18	38	27	22	19	35	23
101-150	17	4	8	8	15	13	13	13
151-200	8	3	0	4	14	9	6	10
201-300	8	0	0	2	19	8	2	10
Over 300	2	1	0	2	18	3	0	7
TOTAL	100	100	100	100	100	100	100	100
Average Sunday congregation (No. of adults morning & evening)	102	46	44	52	182	90	69	108

[1] This table is based on responses from 50% of all Episcopal churches
[2] This table is based on responses from 58% of all Episcopal churches

SCOTTISH EPISCOPAL CHURCH

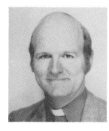

Rev JOHN CLARKE
Information Officer and Communications Adviser, Scottish Episcopal Church

The Scottish Episcopal Church can take some gentle encouragement from the Statistical Survey. During years of considerable change which have seen the introduction of a modern-language Eucharistic Liturgy, a new synodical system of government, the wider development of non-stipendiary ministry and a different marriage discipline, the Episcopal Church has been the only major denomination in Scotland to show an increase in the regular attendance of adults and children.

It would be wise, though, to exercise restraint in interpreting the figures. Whilst overall the numbers are congruent with statistical returns internal to the Episcopal Church, when broken into smaller geographical areas, the size of the sample makes generalisations unreliable. The low response rate of the Church should also be noted.

The survey shows clearly the limited size of the Scottish Episcopal Church. The Episcopal Church membership is 1% of the total adult population and attenders form only 2.4% of adult church attendance in Scotland. There is considerable variation in different parts of Scotland; for

example there are five times as many Episcopalians per head of the population in the Borders as in the Greater Glasgow area. Overall, the Church is much stronger in the East and in rural areas than in more densely populated Strathclyde. Change in attendance mirrors, in most part, the distribution of attenders – where the Episcopal Church is numerically more significant it is growing.

A different pattern is seen in the membership figures, which show an overall decline of 3%. Whilst decline is still most marked in areas where the Church is already small, there are some unexpected regional anomalies. Nevertheless, the Episcopal Church still has a large fringe for a non-established Church, the more so since its own figures suggest that 65,000 people have at least a nominal adherence.

The most remarkable increase in the Census is the 23% increase of children attending Episcopal churches. In spite of this the proportion of children to adults in Episcopal churches is still low compared to the Church of Scotland, the Baptist Church and some other Protestant denominations. What can be hoped is that the change towards greater freedom and active participation within liturgical worship has encouraged both parents and children to perservere in Christian nurture.

Episcopal congregations are small and often scattered. 52 is the average Sunday adult congregation and there are very few that match even the size of the average Church of Scotland attendance. But intimacy may have its advantages, as may the high ratio of ministers (paid and unpaid) to attenders.

What the figures cannot tell us is whether the growth in attendance and decline in membership is evidence of the Episcopal Church's withdrawal into a more demanding and self-conscious sect, or signs of an open and committed Church seeking to proclaim the Kingdom of God in forms appropriate to a divided nation facing a time of economic and social upheaval.

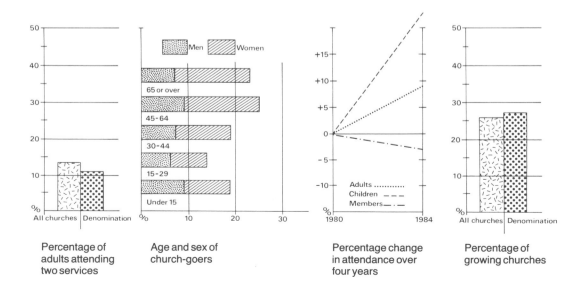

Percentage of adults attending two services

Age and sex of church-goers

Percentage change in attendance over four years

Percentage of growing churches

BAPTIST CHURCHES

Total Adult Population:	3,957,410
Change of adult population in four years:	+1%
Total number of Baptist churches 1984:	186
Percentage of Churches responding:	69%
Total number of Baptist ministers:	169
Percentage of Baptist churches holding mid-week meetings:	98%
Percentage mid-week attendance of Sunday attendance:	24%
1984 adult Baptist church membership as percentage of total adult population:	0.5%
1984 adult Baptist church attenders as percentage of total adult population:	0.5%
1984 adult Baptist church adherents as percentage of total adult population:	0.1%

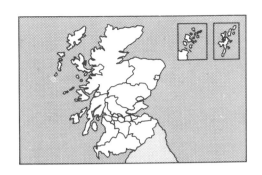

	Child Attenders			Childen under 15 attending Sunday school	Adult Attenders			Adults who attended twice on Sunday	Membership		
	1980	**1984**	Change	1984	1980	**1984**	Change	1984	1980	**1984**	Change
			%	%			%	%			%
Total all churches	209,150	**203,260**	−3	97	677,920	**660,360**	−3	13	1,929,900	**1,876,840**	−3
Baptist	7,910	**7,790**	−2	96	22,280	**21,450**	−4	41	19,220	**20,020**	+4
Percentage Baptist Churches area is of total:	4%	**4%**			3%	**3%**			1%	**1%**	

	Percentage of churches which between 1980 & 1984:			1984 Churches whose services are in:			1984 Churches whose services are in the:		
	Grew	Remained Static	Declined	Gaelic only	Gaelic & English	English only	Morning only	Morn. & Evening	Evening only
	%	%	%	%	%	%	%	%	%
All Churches	26	52	22	½	1½	98	43	53	4
Baptist Churches	38	52	10	0	0	100	1	96	3
Version of Bible most used on Sunday	NIV	NIV	NIV						

	All Church Attenders [1]			All Scottish Protestant Churches		
Age Group	Male	Female	Total	Male	Female	Total
	%	%	%	%	%	%
Under 15	10	14	24	11	14	25
15-19	4	5	9	2	3	5
20-29	7	8	15	3	6	9
30-44	7	10	17	5	10	15
45-64	7	11	18	9	15	24
65 or over	5	12	17	7	15	22
All ages	40	60	100	37	63	100

	Baptist Churches [2]				All Scottish Protestant Churches			
Number Attending Church per week excluding twicers	Growing	Static	Declining	All churches	Growing	Static	Declining	All churches
	%	%	%	%	%	%	%	%
Under 10	0	0	0	0	2	5	4	4
10-25	6	14	14	11	4	17	18	14
26-50	6	21	14	15	6	26	22	19
51-100	31	36	72	38	22	19	35	23
101-150	17	15	0	14	15	13	13	13
151-200	15	8	0	9	14	9	6	10
201-300	13	3	0	6	19	8	2	10
Over 300	12	3	0	7	18	3	0	7
TOTAL	100	100	100	100	100	100	100	100
Average Sunday congregation (No. of adults morning & evening)	154	89	61	117	182	90	69	108

[1] This table is based on responses from 61% of all Baptist churches
[2] This table is based on responses from 69% of all Baptist churches

BAPTIST CHURCHES

Rev PETER BARBER
General Secretary,
Baptist Union of Scotland

Reading these statistics as a Scottish Baptist, one might be excused for a feeling of relief, if not gratification, that the denomination is not faring as badly as the Church in Scotland at large.

It is the only denomination to have advanced in membership over the past four years (4%) and one of only two denominations expected to do so in the next six years (1.2% per annum). It has by far the highest rate of church attendance per membership (107%) and ranks third in terms of the size of the average adult congregation (ie 117 compared with 474 in the Roman Catholic Church and 149 in the Church of Scotland). The number who attend church twice on Sunday is high (41% as against a national average of 13%) and the large proportion of children, young people and the middle-aged is significant. It is also encouraging that the percentage of growing churches (38%) is up on the national average (26%) and that there is a smaller percentage of declining churches (10% as against a national figure of 22%).

Inevitably such statistics must raise the question, why are the Baptists in this exceptional situation?

Part of the reason may lie in the high expectation the Baptist Church has of its members. Personal faith expressed in immersion baptism is expected to lead to responsible Church membership involving sacrificial giving, active service and personal daily witness. These standards, based on the precedent of the New Testament Church, make a strong appeal to the young and not-so-young who have come into an evangelical experience and feel challenged to a wholehearted christian commitment. Perhaps the denomination demonstrates the well-known principle that the more you expect the more you receive.

Other factors must also be taken into account. The smaller size of the congregations (an average of 108 members per church) give a "family feel" to church life. Scripture is kept central in preaching, all-age Christian education and house-group Bible studies. Prayer is given priority. 98% of the churches have a mid-week prayer meeting and there is a recurrent emphasis on private devotions.

Evangelism is also high on the denomination's agenda both nationally and locally. Pioneer ministers have been sent into new areas, financial assistance offered to get new churches under way and an active programme of church planting has been pursued. At the present time 88% of the Baptist Union of Scotland churches are engaged in "Scotreach" – a three year programme of mission initiated by the annual Assembly.

Yet there are anomalies in the statistics that call for some explanation. Why, for instance, are Baptists so sparse in the North West? This no doubt in part reflects the general population drift, but is probably best explained historically. The fact is that when the Haldane brothers led the great missionary advance of the denomination in the 19th century they largely concentrated (as did their missioners) on the South, East and North East, and as they sowed, the denomination still reaps.

The statistics also indicate that in the Baptist Union of Scotland, while membership from 1980-84 increased by 4% the number of adult attenders declined by 1% (4% for all Baptists). Why?

It could be that some, faced by the challenge of committed church membership, shied away. On the other hand it could confirm how right the denomination was in 1984 to set itself the challenge of fresh outreach in the 3-year Scotreach programme.

But the same challenge faces the whole church in Scotland. We simply cannot allow another 64,340 people to drift out of church membership over the next six years. Such haemorrhaging could be fatal and we must somehow stop it by seeking some way of renewal.

Nor can we stop at renewal for its own sake. We will have to be the church renewed *for mission* if we are to take our stewardship of the Gospel seriously and communicate the good news with the 3 million in our land who are now outwith the church altogether.

Arise, let us be going!

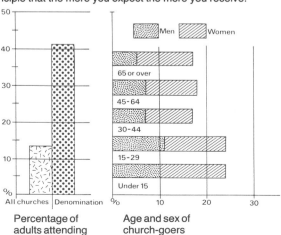

Percentage of
adults attending
two services

Age and sex of
church-goers

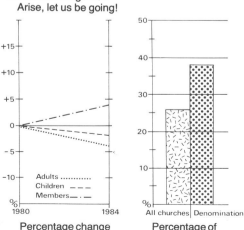

Percentage change
in attendance over
four years

Percentage of
growing churches

INDEPENDENT CHURCHES

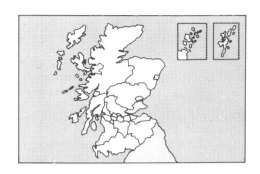

Total Adult Population:	3,957,410
Change of adult population in four years:	+1%
Total number of Independent churches 1984:	438
Percentage of Churches responding:	56%
Total number of Independent ministers:	141
Percentage of Independent churches holding mid-week meetings:	80%
Percentage mid-week attendance of Sunday attendance:	34%
1984 adult Independent church membership as percentage of total adult population:	0.9%
1984 adult Independent church attenders as percentage of total adult population:	0.7%
1984 adult Independent church adherents as percentage of total adult population:	0.1%

	Child Attenders			Children under 15 attending Sunday school	Adult Attenders			Adults who attended twice on Sunday	Membership		
	1980	**1984**	Change	1984	1980	**1984**	Change	1984	1980	**1984**	Change
			%	%			%	%			%
Total all churches	209,150	**203,260**	−3	97	677,920	**990,360**	−3	13	1,929,900	**1,876,840**	−3
Independent	13,250	**12,320**	−7	79	28,130	**27,050**	−4	47	36,620	**35,400**	−3
Percentage Independent Churches are of total:	6%	**6%**			4%	**4%**			2%	**2%**	

	Percentage of churches which between 1980 & 1984:			1984 Churches whose services are in:			1984 Churches whose services are in the:		
	Grew	Remained Static	Declined	Gaelic only	Gaelic & English	English only	Morning only	Morn. & Evening	Evening only
	%	%	%	%	%	%	%	%	%
All Churches	26	52	22	½	1½	98	43	53	4
Independent Churches	18	71	11	0	0	100	20	75	5
Version of Bible most used on Sunday	AV	AV	AV						

	All Church Attenders[1]			All Scottish Protestant Churches		
Age Group	Male	Female	Total	Male	Female	Total
	%	%	%	%	%	%
Under 15	12	16	28	11	14	25
15-19	4	4	8	2	3	5
20-29	4	6	10	3	6	9
30-44	6	8	14	5	10	15
45-64	7	12	19	9	15	24
65 or over	7	14	21	7	15	22
All Ages	40	60	100	37	63	100

Number Attending Church per week excluding twicers	Independent Churches[2]				All Scottish Protestant Churches			
	Growing	Static	Declining	All churches	Growing	Static	Declining	All churches
	%	%	%	%	%	%	%	%
Under 10	0	5	15	5	2	5	4	4
10-25	2	17	8	13	4	17	18	14
26-50	11	36	11	29	6	26	22	19
51-100	47	23	58	31	22	19	35	23
101-150	13	10	4	10	15	13	13	13
151-200	18	7	4	9	14	9	6	10
201-300	9	2	0	3	19	8	2	10
Over 300	0	0	0	0	18	3	0	7
TOTAL	100	100	100	100	100	110	100	100
Average Sunday congregation (No. of adults morning & evening)	110	63	51	61	182	90	69	108

[1] This table is based on responses from 51% of all Independent churches
[2] This table is based on responses from 56% of all Independent churches

INDEPENDENT CHURCHES

Dr ALASTAIR NOBLE
Education Officer,
BBC Scotland

The Independent churches in Scotland, as defined by this census, consist of approximately 300 Christian Brethren churches, 99 Congregational Union churches, and 39 Fellowship of Independent Evangelical Churches (FIEC) and House Churches. These 438 churches account for 11% of all churches in Scotland, and they are attended each Sunday by, on average, 27,000 different adults. This weekly attendance at Independent churches is equivalent to 4% of all church-goers, and only the weekly attendances of the Roman Catholic Church and the Church of Scotland are higher, though considerably so at 44% and 40% of all church-goers respectively. Map 1 shows that the largest concentrations of Independents are in Strathclyde, Central, Fife, Grampian and the city of Edinburgh.

The average Sunday congregation at an Independent church is around 60 (108 is the average for all Protestant Churches), with 47% of the congregation attending twice on Sunday. Of those who attend, 60% are under 45 years of age. Mid-week services are held in 80% of the Independent churches compared with 59% for all churches. Although some caution is required in drawing conclusions from data averaged over groups of Independent churches which have significant differences, the data is consistent with churches of manageable size, with a significant proportion of young people and young

marrieds, and where there is a high level of commitment and fellowship. The fact that the 438 Independent churches have only 141 ministers is accounted for by the 300 Christian Brethren churches which have no ministers, and indicates a high level of lay leadership and responsibility.

Independent church members form 2% of all Scottish church members, and membership and attendance can be further analysed as shown in the table below.

Overall attendance is declining, at 4% over the four years 1980-84, which is slightly greater than the 3% decline for all Protestant churches. The 3% decline in membership is less than the 5% decline for all Protestant churches, and is accounted for entirely by the drop in membership of the Congregational Union. The overall membership of Christian Brethren, FIEC and House Churches has remained static over the four years 1980-84. The weekly attendance at these churches is, on average, 2% higher than the total membership, whereas average attendance at Congregational Union churches is equivalent to only 51% of the membership.

Map 2 shows that some growth is occurring in the Borders, in Lothian outside Edinburgh and in Tayside outside Dundee, areas where the Independents are relatively weak. There is also growth in Grampian, where they are relatively strong. However the areas where attendance is declining include Strathclyde where they have their greatest strength. Another point of concern is that although the 7% drop in child attenders is in line with the 8% drop in the child population, it is significantly worse than the drop of 3% for all churches.

The data points to a number attractive and encouraging features about the independent churches, but also gives an overall picture of gentle decline. The Independent churches are a significant part of the Scottish church scene, but a group which, on these figures, cannot afford to be complacent.

Independent Churches sub-groups	Adult Attenders		Members		Number of Churches 1984
	1984	1980-84 change	1984	1980-84 change	
Christian Brethren/FIEC/ House Churches	18,170	− 4%	17,840	0%	339
Congregational Union	8,880	− 3%	17,560	− 7%	99
Total	27,050	− 4%	35,400	− 3%	438

Independent Attendance Strength

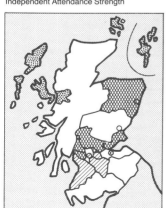

Less than 500 in 1984
Between 500 and 1,000
Between 1,001 and 2,000
Over 2,000

Independent Attendance Change 1980-84

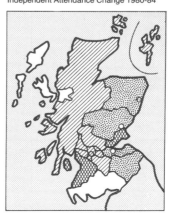

Growth rate 5% or more
Growth rate up to 5%
Decline rate up to − 5%
Decline rate more than − 5%

See Page 105 for additional diagrams for Independent Churches

OTHER DENOMINATIONS

Total Adult Population:	3,957,410
Change of adult population in four years:	+1%
Total number of Other Denominations churches 1984:	445
Percentage of Churches responding:	83%
Total number of Other Denominations ministers:	518
Percentage of Other Denominations churches holding mid-week meetings:	67%
Percentage mid-week attendance of Sunday attendance:	18%
1984 adult Other Denominations church membership as percentage of total adult population:	0.9%
1984 adult Other Denominations church attenders as percentage of total adult population:	0.6%
1984 adult Other Denominations church adherents as percentage of total adult population:	0.3%

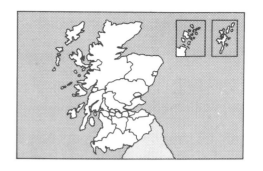

	Child Attenders 1980	Child Attenders 1984	Change	Childen under 15 attending Sunday school 1984	Adult Attenders 1980	Adult Attenders 1984	Change	Adults who attended twice on Sunday 1984	Membership 1980	Membership 1984	Change
			%	%			%	%			%
Total all churches	209,150	**203,260**	−3	97	677,920	**660,360**	−3	13	1,929,900	**1,876,840**	−3
Other Denominations	10,910	**11,140**	+2	97	25,360	**25,610**	+1	34	35,510	**34,310**	−3
Percentage Other Denominations are of total:	5%	**5%**			4%	**4%**			2%	**2%**	

	Percentage of churches which between 1980 & 1984: Grew	Remained Static	Declined	1984 Churches whose services are in: Gaelic only	Gaelic & English	English only	1984 Churches whose services are in the: Morning only	Morn. & Evening	Evening only
	%	%	%	%	%	%	%	%	%
All Churches	26	52	22	½	1½	98	43	53	4
Other Denominations	26	65	9	0	0	100	28	62	10
Version of Bible most used on Sunday	AV	AV	AV						

Age Group	All Church Attenders[1] Male	Female	Total	All Scottish Protestant Churches Male	Female	Total
	%	%	%	%	%	%
Under 15	11	15	26	11	14	25
15-19	3	4	7	2	3	5
20-29	4	6	10	3	6	9
30-44	6	9	15	5	10	15
45-64	7	13	20	9	15	24
65 or over	7	15	22	7	15	22
All ages	38	62	100	37	63	100

Number Attending Church per week excluding twicers	Other Denominations[2] Growing	Static	Declining	All churches	All Scottish Protestant Churches Growing	Static	Declining	All churches
	%	%	%	%	%	%	%	%
Under 10	9	11	23	12	2	5	4	4
10-25	13	27	19	22	4	17	18	14
26-50	20	32	16	28	6	26	22	19
51-100	36	18	32	24	22	19	35	23
101-150	18	9	7	11	15	13	13	13
151-200	1	1	3	1	14	9	6	10
201-300	3	2	0	2	19	8	2	10
Over 300	0	0	0	0	18	3	0	7
TOTAL	100	100	100	100	100	100	100	100
Average Sunday congregation (No. of adults morning & evening)	68	47	48	58	182	90	69	108

[1] This table is based on responses from 76% of all Other Denominations churches
[2] This table is based on responses from 82% of all Other Denominations churches

OTHER DENOMINATIONS

Mrs ELSIE MOULT
Vice-President of the Methodist Conference 1980-81; Vice-President of the British Council of Churches

'*Other Denominations*' includes the Salvation Army, the United Free, Methodist, Pentecostal Churches and fourteen smaller Churches. Attempting to comment on figures of all these together must be either crazy or arrogant. Their scattering over wide areas of Scotland or their non-existence in others, creates special problems. The movement of a couple of families, in or out, can affect the life of a church. The wide variety of situations makes meaningful analysis problematic.

'Other Denominations' have lost 3% in membership, matching a similar loss in all other churches. This percentage hides great variation in increases and decreases among the denominations and in different areas. In Strathclyde, for instance, in the movement of people from inner city areas (Glasgow's population has fallen 7%), smaller denominations closed churches and in the new areas people joined churches near to new homes.

Some denominations did not follow their members to new areas (probably lack of resources) and perhaps in these ecumenical days, they should not.

Movement of people, from other parts of Britain and the world, to work in oil and its related industries (e.g. Aberdeen) has boosted some denominations – while similiar movement into areas where these denominations do not exist, has meant loss.

Some churches have deliberately trimmed their membership figures to present a realistic picture of the participating congregation.

Few churches have been untouched by the charismatic movement. It is not surprising, therefore, that the Pentecostal Churches, for whom this is their ethos, have increased in membership.

It is noted that while there is a 3% decrease in membership, there is a 1% increase in adult attendance. Hearteningly, this keeps face with the increase in Scotland's population. People seem to be attending churches, who do not wish to make the commitment which membership implies, or feel that membership is not a priority for Christian witness. There is concern and challenge in this situation.

2% increase in Child Attenders brings a little satisfaction at a time of decrease in the child population and the Churches' anxiety about declining work among children. 'Other Denominations' are a little better at retaining young people of 15-29 age groups than other Protestant Churches, but percentages are so small that there is little cause for complacency.

Lutheran and Orthodox Churches, along with others in this group, are reminders of large communions of the World Church. Bringing their own ethos and insights, they enrich the whole Church in Scotland.

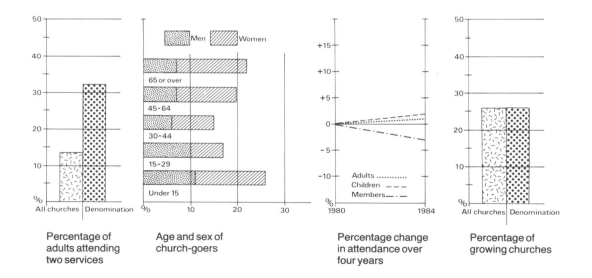

Percentage of adults attending two services

Age and sex of church-goers

Percentage change in attendance over four years

Percentage of growing churches

ROMAN CATHOLIC CHURCH

Total Adult Population:	3,957,410
Change of adult population in four years:	+1%
Total number of Roman Catholic churches 1984:	606
Percentage of Churches responding:	69%
Total number of Roman Catholic priests:	1,134
Percentage of Roman Catholic churches holding mid-week meetings:	45%
Percentage mid-week attendance of Sunday attendance:	2%
1984 Roman Catholic church membership as percentage of total adult population:	20%
1984 adult Roman Catholic church attenders as percentage of total adult population:	7.3%
1984 adult Roman Catholic church adherents as percentage of total adult population:	0%

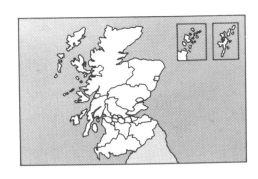

	Child Attenders			Children under 15 attending Sunday school	Adult Attenders			Adults who attended twice on Sunday	Membership		
	1980	**1984**	Change	1984	1980	**1984**	Change	1984	1980	**1984**	Change
			%	%		**%**	%	%			%
Total all churches	209,150	**203,260**	−3	97	677,920	**660,360**	−3	13	1,929,900	**1,876,840**	−3
Roman Catholic	71,050	**68,880**	−3	n/a[5]	296,030	**286,990**	−3	3	816,100[3]	**814,400[3]**	0
Percentage Roman Catholics are of total :	34%	**34%**			44%	**44%**			42%	**43%**	

	Percentage of churches which between 1980 & 1984:			1984 Churches whose services are in:			1984 Churches whose services are in the:		
	Grew	Remained Static	Declined	Gaelic only	Gaelic & English	English only	Morning only	Morn. & Evening	Evening only
	%	%	%	%	%	%	%	%	%
All Churches	26	52	22	½	1½	98	43	53	4
Roman Catholic	20	56	24	½	½	99	25	73	2
Version of Bible most used on Sunday	JER	JER	JER						

	All Church Attenders[1]			All Scottish Protestant Churches		
Age Group	Male	Female	Total	Male	Female	Total
	%	%	%	%	%	%
Under 15	11	13	24	11	14	25
15-19	3	4	7	2	3	5
20-29	5	8	13	3	6	9
30-44	7	10	17	5	10	15
45-64	9	13	22	9	15	24
65 or over	8	9	17	7	15	22
All ages	43	57	100	37	63	100

	Roman Catholic Churches[2]				All Scottish Churches [4]			
Number Attending Church per week excluding twicers	Growing	Static	Declining	All churches	Growing	Static	Declining	All churches
	%	%	%	%	%	%	%	%
Under 10	1	2	1	2	2	4	4	4
10-25	0	4	7	4	4	15	16	12
26-50	0	5	6	4	5	23	20	17
51-100	10	8	10	9	21	18	31	21
101-150	18	6	3	8	15	12	11	13
151-200	5	4	5	4	13	8	6	9
201-300	5	9	16	9	18	8	4	10
Over 300	61	62	52	60	22	12	8	14
TOTAL	100	100	100	100	100	100	100	100
Average Sunday congregation (No. of adults morning & evening	576	516	392	474	176	110	90	163

[1] This table is based on special surveys of 4% of all Roman Catholic churches
[2] This table is based on responses from 66% of all Roman Catholic churches
[3] Total Catholic population including children
[4] Protestant and Roman Catholic
[5] This question was not asked on Roman Catholic forms

THE ROMAN CATHOLIC CHURCH

Rt Rev JOSEPH DEVINE,
Bishop of Motherwell

Since 1981 the Catholic Church in Scotland has conducted an annual survey of all those attending Mass on the first Sunday in November. The result, based upon 100% parish returns, is in the form of an *overall total* since it is extremely difficult to establish the numbers in the various age groupings which has been a most significant achievement of this survey. The reason for the difficulty is self-explanatory. The average number attending a Catholic Church on a Sunday is 474. The next highest average attendance is that of the Church of Scotland at 149. However, an attempt has been made to estimate the numbers in each age group within the overall total. In my estimation there is a quite credible degree of accuracy in all of those suggested figures.

But credible accuracy yields to fact in relation to the overall total. That total is based upon a 69% parish return in this survey. The conclusion to which the survey points is given striking confirmation by the fact that the Catholic Church's own statistical survey for 1984 produces a conclusion which is not significantly dissimilar. Such independent evidence gives a powerful indication of the likely accuracy of the survey in all its findings.

But facts are one thing and interpretation another. It is a matter of some importance to recognise that it is baptism which establishes membership within the Roman Catholic Church rather than being on a Communicants' Roll or after commitment ceremonies as an adult. In addition, on each Catholic there is laid the obligation of attending Mass on a Sunday. Other Christian denominations may not require such regularity of practice. As a consequence, Roman Catholic attendance figures, as a percentage of the total membership, have to be interpreted carefully and never more so than when being contrasted with attendance figures for other Christian Churches. Even greater care must be taken when drawing comparisons between the numbers in the various age groups.

But that reservation apart, I am in no doubt about the value of this survey. Its findings should be studied closely by Church leaders and given serious attention in the pastoral thinking of the near future. If the truth is sometimes unpalatable this survey also contains a great deal of evidence which suggests that there are considerable strengths within the Churches. That strength will need to be harnessed for the work of mission and evangelisation. Both the unchurched and the lapsed must be the major item on the pastoral agenda of the Churches for the future.

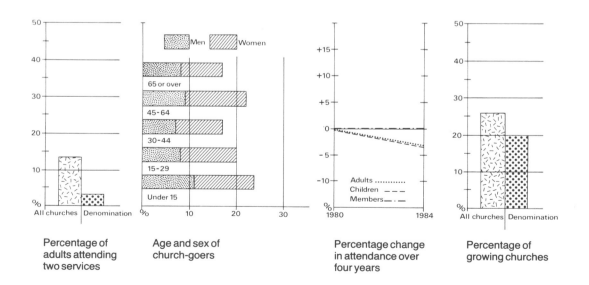

Percentage of adults attending two services

Age and sex of church-goers

Percentage change in attendance over four years

Percentage of growing churches

PATTERNS OF MORNING & EVENING ATTENDANCE

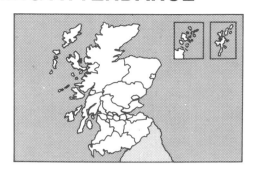

Total number of Churches 1984:	4,063
Percentage of Churches responding:	75%
Total number of Church of Scotland churches 1984:	1,790
Total number of Roman Catholic churches 1984:	606

	Percentage of Churches whose services in 1980 were held:			Percentage of Churches whose services in 1984 were held:			Percentage of Attenders in 1980 who went:			Percentage of Attenders in 1984 who went:		
	Morning only	Morning and Evening	Evening only	Morning only	Morning and Evening	Evening only	Morning only	Morning and Evening	Evening only	Morning only	Morning and Evening	Evening only
	%	%	%	%	%	%	%	%	%	%	%	%
All Churches	**20**	**77**	**3**	**43**	**53**	**4**	**59**	**12**	**29**	**61**	**13**	**26**
Church of Scotland	19	80	1	59	40	1	74	12	14	74	11	15
Conservative Presbyterian	10	77	13	12	72	16	25	51	24	25	51	24
Scottish Episcopal	53	44	3	59	38	3	79	12	9	78	11	11
Baptist	3	94	3	1	96	3	45	40	15	43	41	16
Independent	12	86	2	20	75	5	30	50	20	34	47	19
Other Denominations	18	73	9	28	62	10	38	40	22	39	34	27
Roman Catholic	20	79	1	25	73	2	61	4	35	61	3	36
Borders	30	70	0	66	33	1	64	16	20	63	19	18
Central	19	81	0	45	55	0	67	13	20	70	12	18
Dumfries and Galloway	31	68	1	68	31	1	66	13	21	67	13	20
Fife	22	76	2	48	50	2	62*	9*	29*	68	13	19
Grampian: Aberdeen	17	80	3	39	57	4	65	17	18	66	18	16
Grampian: Other	24	71	5	54	38	8	52*	25*	23	61	17	22
Highland excluding Skye & Lochalsh but including Argyll & Bute	22	73	5	41	52	7	56	27	17	60	23	17
Lothian: Edinburgh	19	78	3	44	53	3	69	13	18	68	16	16
Lothian: Other	30	70	0	52	47	1	69	7	24	66	10	24
Orkney Islands	23	74	3	50	47	3	2*	56*	42*	53	32	15
Shetland Islands	15	60	25	30	44	26	35	40	25	38	37	25
Strathclyde: Dumbarton, Clydebank and Cumbernauld & Kilsyth	14	86	0	35	65	0	56	19*	25*	54	7	39
Strathclyde: East Kilbride, Hamilton & Lanark	19	81	0	36	64	0	53	9	38	57	11	32
Strathclyde: Eastwood, Bearsden & Milngavie, and Strathkelvin	11	89	0	31	69	0	60	8	32	59	9	32
Strathclyde: Glasgow	11	87	2	25	72	3	52	10	38	59	9	32
Strathclyde: Kyle & Carrick, Cumnoch & Doun Valley, Kilmarnock & Loudon, and Cunninghame	22	77	1	43	56	1	58	15	27	60	16	24
Strathclyde: Motherwell and Monklands	14	85	1	26	73	1	55	8	37	59	7	34
Strathclyde: Renfrew & Inverclyde	7	93	0	26	74	0	66	10	24	68	11	21
Tayside: Dundee	23	76	1	46	52	2	60	18	22	68	16	16
Tayside: Other	24	71	5	68	27	5	64	25*	11*	62	17	21
Western Isles & Skye & Lochalsh	11	78	11	16	68	16	20	49	31	27	43	30

* Percentages unreliable because based on particularly small numbers

52

PATTERNS OF MORNING AND EVENING ATTENDANCE

Rev ALASTAIR MORRICE
Church of Scotland
Holy Trinity, Edinburgh

There has been a remarkable drop in the number of churches holding evening services from 77% of all churches in 1980 to 53% in 1984.

Does this mean the end of the evening service?

Many ministers and members had come by 1980 to feel that a second diet of worship was not a necessary component in their spiritual growth. Many ministers were being put under greater pressure on Sundays, especially in the Church of Scotland, by the progress of policies of Union and Readjustment, which greatly increased the number of services conducted by one minister in different locations.

At the same time economic reasons were influencing office bearers. Increases in the price of fuel and other costs put pressure upon the least well-attended service.

In contexts where a vital spiritual hunger was missing such pressures proved irresistible. In many places it was the Kirk Session itself which "closed the door", elders themselves declaring that they did not want to be involved in evening worship.

Can we suggest reasons for such a drastic decline?

It is interesting to note that whereas the number of services decreased by 24%, the proportion of attenders coming twice has actually increased overall by 1%, even in the Church of Scotland only decreasing by 1%.

It is arguable why this should be so. It would be interesting to find out from all ministers holding evening services why they continue. Would their response indicate that many of these ministers see the evening service as an additional opportunity to bring God's Word to their people in a less hurrried and cluttered context? If that were so and the Word of God itself were coming alive in congregations where vital commitment was growing then it might explain the maintenance of good figures for new and continuing evening services against an overall large decrease in the opportunities for such worship.

A tendency to growth is demonstrable where churches have desire and opportunity to meet twice a Sunday and mid-week. In churches where this happens 29% were growing, 55% were static and only 16% declining (as against those which had morning services only whose corresponding figures were 23%, 48%, 29%).

The figures, therefore, do not prove that the day of the evening service is over. The decline may be near its nadir and the growing churches may increasingly be those whose commitment is represented by a desire to meet more than once a week under the living Word of God.

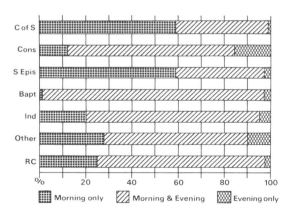

Proportion of church-goers by time(s) of attendance.

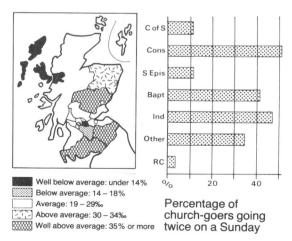

Well below average: under 14%
Below average: 14 – 18%
Average: 19 – 29‰
Above average: 30 – 34‰
Well above average: 35% or more

Percentage of church-goers going twice on a Sunday

Proportion of Churches which have gone from two Sunday Services in 1980 to one service by 1984

THE USE OF THE GAELIC LANGUAGE

Total number of churches 1984:	4,063
Percentage of Churches responding:	*75%*
Total 1980 adult church attenders:	677,920
Total 1984 adult church attenders:	660,360

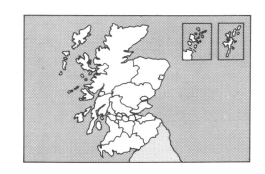

	Adult Attenders in Churches in 1980 using:			Adult Attenders in Churches in 1984 using:			Percentage of churches with Gaelic and/or Gaelic & English Services in	
	Gaelic only	Gaelic and English	English only	Gaelic only	Gaelic and English	English only	1980	1984
							%	%
All Churches	**2,490**	**14,900**	**660,530**	**2,150**	**12,620**	**645,590**	*2*	*2*
Church of Scotland	150	4,970	267,540	130	4,160	262,010	*2*	*2*
Conservative Presbyterian	2,140	9,570	9,040	1,830	8,080	7,220	*19*	*18*
Scottish Episcopal	0	130	14,400	0	140	15,690	*1*	*1*
Baptist	0	0	22,280	0	0	21,450	*0*	*0*
Independent	0	0	28,130	0	0	27,050	*0*	*0*
Other Denominations	0	0	25,360	0	0	25,610	*0*	*0*
Roman Catholic	200	230	295,600	190	240	286,560	*1*	*1*
Borders	0	0	9,610	0	0	10,400	*0*	*0*
Central	0	210	29,270	0	210	29,330	*1*	*1*
Dumfries and Galloway	0	0	15,080	0	0	15,640	*0*	*0*
Fife	0	0	30,840	0	0	30,830	*0*	*0*
Grampian: Aberdeen	0	0	15,960	0	0	15,190	*0*	*0*
Grampian: Other	0	0	26,370	0	0	27,670	*0*	*0*
Highland excluding Skye & Lochalsh but including Argyll & Bute	0	510	31,640	0	630	32,540	*2*	*2*
Lothian: Edinburgh	0	300	45,190	0	320	41,720	*1*	*1*
Lothian: Other	0	0	30,600	0	0	28,330	*0*	*0*
Orkney Islands	0	0	2,060	0	0	2,070	*0*	*0*
Shetland Islands	0	0	2,510	0	0	2,500	*0*	*0*
Strathclyde: Dumbarton, Clydebank and Cumbernauld & Kilsyth	0	0	32,960	0	0	34,110	*0*	*0*
Strathclyde: East Kilbride, Hamilton & Lanark	0	0	35,420	0	0	35,660	*0*	*0*
Strachclyde: Eastwood, Bearsden & Milngavie, and Strathkelvin	0	0	25,560	0	0	27,650	*0*	*0*
Strathclyde: Glasgow	0	950	123,890	0	990	114,720	*1*	*1*
Strathclyde: Kyle & Carrick, Cumnoch & Doun Valley, Kilmarnock & Loudon, and Cunninghame	0	0	49,100	0	0	48,020	*0*	*0*
Strathclyde: Motherwell and Monklands	0	0	56,840	0	0	54,350	*0*	*0*
Strathclyde: Renfrew & Inverclyde	0	0	56,480	0	0	53,270	*0*	*0*
Tayside: Dundee	0	0	17,900	0	0	17,760	*0*	*0*
Tayside: Other	0	0	20,070	0	0	19,650	*0*	*0*
Western Isles and Skye & Lochalsh & Lochalsh	2,490	12,930	3,130	2,150	10,470	4,180	*57*	*54*

THE USE OF THE GAELIC LANGUAGE

**Rev Professor
DONALD MACLEOD**
*Professor of Systematic
Theology at the Free
Church College, and
Editor of "The Monthly
Record"*

The Gaelic statistics contain several striking features.

One is that the vast majority of Gaelic-speaking attenders are to be found in the Conservative Presbyterian churches: 1,830 attending Gaelic-only churches and 8,080 attending Gaelic/English churches. The only other body which comes close to these figures is the Church of Scotland with a mere 130 attenders in Gaelic-only churches and 4,160 in Gaelic/English ones.

Another is the fact that 2,490 people are attending Gaelic-only churches. This is all the more remarkable when one remembers that in the Western Isles many of the Gaelic/English churches have only a minimal number of English services. In some areas the "regular use of both languages in worship" may mean only that there is one English service a month. Unless one speaks Gaelic, on most Sundays in the year there is simply no church service to attend. This is surely a significant factor in the overall decline in church attendance among Conservative Presbyterians, the main Gaelic denominations.

One is also struck by the position of Gaelic in the Roman Catholic and Episcopal churches. 190 Roman Catholic adults attend Gaelic-only churches. On the other hand the general provision for Gaelic in this communion is limited. Out of a total of 1,560 adult attenders in the Western Isles, Skye and Lochalsh, Gaelic is available for only 430. The

figures for the Scottish Episcopal Church make one's eyes pop: bilingual provision for 140, whereas the total adult attendance for the Western Isles, Skye and Lochalsh is only 180.

But the most striking feature of all is the drop in Gaelic-speaking adults attending church. The figures as published suggest that there will be no Gaelic-speakers in any church by 2003. The plight of Gaelic is related, of course, to the plight of the smaller Presbyterian churches. According to the census, the decline in these churches is the largest of any group in a four-year period in Scotland, England or Wales: and the Western Isles is the area with the fastest rate of decline in church attendance anywhere in the UK.

For anyone interested in the Gaelic areas, the Conservative Presbyterian churches or the Western Isles these figures are not simply alarming. They are devastating.

But are they accurate? According to official Free Church of Scotland figures, the number of communicants in the main Gaelic-speaking areas fell only slightly between 1980 and 1983 (from 2,594 to 2,534, a drop of 2.3%). According to figures lodged with the Free Presbytery of Lewis, morning attendances between 1980 and 1983 rose from 3,353 and evening attendances rose from 4,048 to 4,397. The underlying trend in the number of communicants in the same presbytery also appears to be upwards. It rose from 2,085 in 1983 to 2,127 in 1984.

The figures for the Gaelic areas are so demoralising, so contrary to expectations and so different from official figures lodged elsewhere that it would be irresponsible to draw any conclusions from them. The base-line is uncertain: local methods of calculating were variable and unprofessional; the month of March is a highly atypical one in the Western Isles; and at the time of the survey 4 of the largest Gaelic congregations (the Free Churches of Knock, Park, Lochs and Stornoway) were without pastors.

There is good objective evidence that problems are beginning to appear in the church-life of the Gaelic-speaking areas. But despondency on the scale suggested by these figures would be premature. It might also, unfortunately, be self-fulfilling.

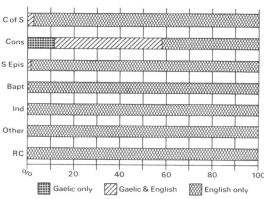

Proportion of church-goers by language of service.

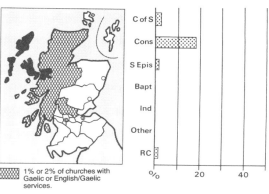

Proportion of churches with Gaelic or Gaelic/English services.

MID-WEEK MEETINGS

Total number of Churches 1984: 4,063

Percentage of Churches responding: 75%

Total number of Church of Scotland churches 1984: 1,790

Total number of Roman Catholic churches 1984: 606

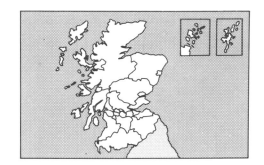

	All churches			Church of Scotland			Roman Catholic[1]	
	Churches with mid-week meetings	Average attendance	Bible Version most used	Churches with mid-week meetings	Average attendance	Bible Version most used	Churches with mid-week meetings	Average attendance
	%			%			%	
All Churches	59	20	AV					
Church of Scotland	53	16	GNB	53	16	GNB		
Conservative Presbyterian	64	19	AV					
Scottish Episcopal	54	12	GNB					
Baptist	98	29	NIV					
Independent	80	27	AV					
Other Denominations	67	17	AV					
Roman Catholic	45	32	JER				45	32
Borders	45	12	RSV	32	11	NEB/RSV	50	9
Central	62	16	GNB	62	14	GNB	30	18
Dumfries and Galloway	43	14	AV	41	13	GNB	25	11
Fife	59	18	GNB	48	15	GNB	48	11
Grampian: Aberdeen	59	26	GNB	53	21	GNB	38	26
Grampian: Other	44	17	GNB	38	14	GNB	44	12
Highland excluding Skye & Lochalsh but including Argyll & Bute	59	14	AV	62	12	GNB	49	19
Lothian: Edinburgh	67	23	AV	64	20	NEB	54	19
Lothian: Other	58	17	GNB	57	12	GNB	34	33
Orkney Islands	52	17	AV	39	17	AV	*	*
Shetland Islands	60	16	AV	69	11	Various	0	–
Strathclyde: Dumbarton, Clydebank and Cumbernauld & Kilsyth	70	25	GNB	67	19	GNB	50	63
Strathclyde: East Kilbride, Hamilton & Lanark	65	25	AV	56	18	GNB	43	27
Strathclyde: Eastwood, Bearsden & Milngavie, and Strathkelvin	81	21	GNB	86	20	GNB	25	10
Strathclyde: Glasgow	66	30	GNB	69	19	GNB	43	81
Strathclyde: Kyle & Carrick, Cumnoch & Doun Valley, Kilmarnock & Loudon, and Cunninghame	57	21	AV	49	18	NEB	57	22
Strathclyde: Motherwell and Monklands	64	24	AV	64	21	GNB	52	29
Strathclyde: Renfrew & Inverclyde	66	19	GNB	55	17	GNB	60	26
Tayside: Dundee	59	19	GNB	40	18	GNB	69	18
Tayside: Other	45	13	AV	32	12	GNB	29	13
Western Isles and Skye & Lochalsh	67	25	AV	82	32	AV	43	10

[1] Bible version not shown as it is always the Jerusalem Bible, except in the Eastwood, Bearsden & Milngavie, and Strathkelvin part of Strathclyde where the GNB is equally used
* Too few churches to give a meaningful figure

MID-WEEK MEETINGS

Rev GEORGE M PHILIP
*Minister, Sandyford
Henderson Memorial
Church, Glasgow*

A glance at chart 1, which shows the proportion of churches in each denomination holding mid-week meetings, may well cause many to ask in surprise where all these meetings are to be found, as the general public seems unaware of their existence.

The census only asked whether a church had any form of service/meeting/group to study the Bible, apart from on Sunday, so the meetings may well be very varied: held in church, hall or house, during afternoon or evening, and for the purpose of Bible Study, prayer, communion, mass, healing or fellowship. But variety in the type of meeting is surely not the main reason why many are unaware that the church holds mid-week meetings. More significant is the fact of the small numbers who attend. The returns from most areas show an average attendance of less than 20 while in some groups the average is as low as 8.

The mid-week figures must be considered in the light of general membership and attendance. Chart 2 shows the proportion of church members who go to the mid-week meeting and Chart 3 the total numbers involved.

Taking all the churches together, only 3% of the membership attends a mid-week meeting. Although the Baptists and Independents each have 25%, the Church of Scotland and Roman Catholics have only 2% and 1% respectively.

Only a very small proportion of Sunday attenders and an almost negligible proportion of nominal members appear to have a sufficiently strong and personal religious interest to cause them to see the need for religious involvement during the week. This highlights the colossal amount of nominal church memberhsip.

On the whole denominations with a more rigorously held position on Biblical doctrine and church discipline hold more mid-week meetings than others, though this is not the case with the Roman Catholics. Of course there are individual congregations in various denominations with well attended weekly meetings which are lost sight of in 'average' figures.

There does seem to be a positive connection between meeting mid-week and growth in the church. Some Baptist and Independent churches record over a 50% growth and *all* of these have a mid-week meeting. Also where the AV or the NIV is used a higher proportion of churches have such a meeting than where other versions are used. Does this suggest that the choice of the AV or NIV implies a readiness to work at Bible Study?

The most searching comment on these statistics may be that the nature of meetings may be more important than their number. Are they committed to Scripture as the Word of God in its full authority? Do they have a significant element of intercessory prayer? "If my people pray . . . " (2 Chron 7:14) is still the vital issue for God's people.

**Fig 1   Proportion of churches which have some
mid-week meetings**

**Fig 2   Proportion of church members who attend
mid-week meetings**

**Fig 3   Total number of members attending
mid-week meetings**

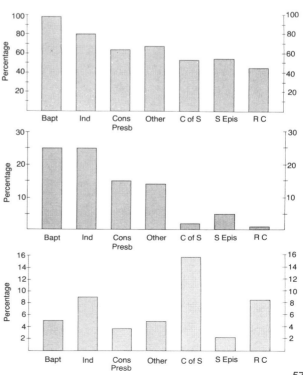

ALL SCOTLAND 1990 PROJECTION

Total 1990 Adult Population:	4,101,000
Change per annum of adult population:	+0.5%
Total number of churches:	3,980
Total number of ministers:	3,530
1990 adult Protestant church membership as percentage of total adult population:	24%
1990 Roman Catholic church membership as percentage of total adult population:	20%
1990 adult church attenders (Protestant and Roman Catholic) as percentage of total adult population:	16%
1990 adult chuch adherents as percentage of total adult population:	2%

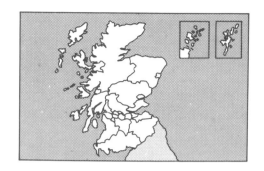

	Adult Attenders			Annual rate of change of Attenders		Membership			Annual rate of change of Members	
	1980	1984	1990	1980-84	1984-90	1980	1984	1990	1980-84	1984-90
				%	%				%	%
Church of Scotland	272,660	266,300	259,000	−0.6	−0.4	953,940	907,920	844,500	−1.2	−1.2
Conservative Presbyterian	18,930	17,130	15,000	−2.5	−2.2	27,550[1]	25,180[1]	22,500[1]	−2.2	−1.8
Scottish Episcopal	14,530	15,830	18,500	+2.2	+2.7	40,960	39,610	38,000	−0.8	−0.6
Baptist	22,280	21,450	21,000	−0.9	−0.3	19,220	20,020	21,500	+1.0	+1.2
Independent	28,130	27,050	26,000	−1.0	−0.5	36,620	35,400	34,000	−0.8	−0.6
Other Denominations	25,360	25,610	26,500	+0.2	+0.6	35,510	34,310	33,000	−0.9	−0.7
TOTAL Protestant	381,890	373,370	366,000	−0.6	−0.4	1,113,800	1,062,440	993,500	−1.2	−1.1
Roman Catholic	296,030	286,990	278,200	−0.8	−0.5	816,100[2]	814,400[2]	819,000[2]	0	+0.1
TOTAL All Churches	677,920	660,360	644,200	−0.7	−0.4	1,929,900	1,876,840	1,812,500	−0.7	−0.6

These tentative figures show the situation as it will be in 1990, if the churches continue to move in the next six years as they did between 1980 and 1984.

Adult Population calculated for Scotland using OPCS projections 1971 to 1981, with 1979 base.

Number of churches and ministers. The *UK Christian Handbook 1985/86* edition quotes the number of churches and ministers in Scotland in 1980. The rate of change for the country as a whole 1980-1984 was applied to each denomination individually and totalled.

Membership and attendance. Figures quoted are based on projections of each denominational group's figures in each area, ar summed nationally.

[1] Conservative Presbyterian adherents are included with members
[2] Total Catholic population including children

FUTURE TRENDS: PROJECTION TO 1990 FOR ALL SCOTLAND

**Rev Canon
KENYON E WRIGHT**
*General Secretary,
Scottish Churches
Council*

If we are to use this painstaking survey as it deserves – in a way that will be useful to the Churches in the years ahead – we must from the start be clear what it does tell us and what it does not. It gives us figures, the statistics and trends in Church attendance and membership in Scotland, with massive documentation, scientifically accurate methods, and great integrity. It tells us more or less what we knew already by impression and feeling, with a few interesting surprises.

If however we are to proceed beyond examination, to diagnosis and prescription, we must recognise the limits of this method. It does not, taken alone, tell us what God is doing in Scotland. There is for example no assessment whatever of the tremendous growth of co-operative and ecumenical work in the Churches – of the Councils of Churches, national and local, which are of growing importance in the Church's ministry (I detect an interesting hint of correlation between the areas of growth, and the degree of ecumenical interest and concern – but this is only an impression). It makes no attempt to assess the quality of the Church's mission, the influence of the Church in community affairs, the growth of new forms of Church life, worship, and ministry. The churches are not competing supermarkets selling religion; they are the people of God within the nation and human history. The Church's past is littered with examples to show that statistics alone cannot diagnose even the health of the Church, still less the Kingdom of God.

Future trends are not simply the projection of figures, but the acceptance of prophetic choices. Used aright, this survey provides us with an excellent opportunity and stimulus to do the right things and ask the right questions. Let us not, for God's sake, rush back into our denominational ghettoes (even the largest Churches are clearly minorities) to wring our hands in horror, to issue our urgent statements and calls, to plan our evangelistic campaigns. Let us rather quietly pray and discuss *together* in order to identify what God is saying to us in Scotland today through this survey and other evidence – and be prepared together to look at all aspects of our common mission and service. Are we ready, locally and nationally, to give up the vested interests which more effectively keep us apart than any theological questions, and together to plan our resources with a common understanding of God's call to us, in which evangelism, mission, service and prophetic witness all have their proper place? If we are not, we will continue to decline in relevance and probably in numbers. If we do use this opportunity for renewed common prayer and planning, then we may or may not increase in numbers, but we will be the salt, the leaven, the city set on the hill. This survey sheds further light, to add to the light of the Gospel already showing up our Churches and our nation for what they are. There is light enough if we are ready to see. Our problem is not light, it is obedience.

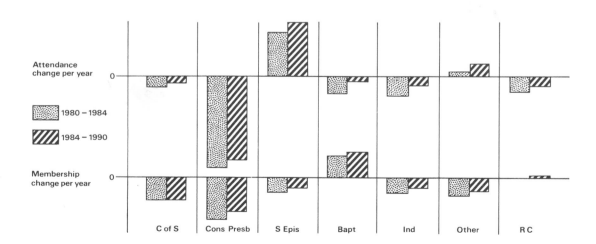

SCOTLAND: TOTAL

Total Adult Population:	3,957,410
Change of adult population in four years:	+1%
Total child population (under 15):	1,077,940
Change of child population in four years:	−8%
Total number of churches:	4,063
Percentage of churches responding:	75%
Total number of ministers:	3,766
Percentage of churches holding mid-week meetings:	59%
1984 adult Protestant church membership as percentage of total adult population:	27%
1984 Roman Catholic church membership as percentage of total adult population:	20%
1984 adult church attenders (Protestant and Roman Catholic) as percentage of total adult population:	17%
1984 adult church adherents as percentage of total adult population:	2%

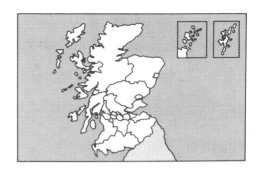

	Child Attenders			Adult Attenders			Membership			Average Sunday Congregation[1]
	1980	1984	Change	1980	1984	Change	1980	1984	Change	1984
			%			%			%	Adults
Church of Scotland	98,360	**95,040**	−3	272,660	**266,300**	−2	953,940	**907,920**	−5	149
Conservative Presbyterian	4,280	**3,920**	−8	18,930	**17,130**	−9	27,550[4]	**25,180[4]**	−9	59
Scottish Episcopal	3,390	**4,170**	+23	14,530	**15,830**	+9	40,960	**39,610**	−3	52
Baptist	7,910	**7,790**	−2	22,280	**21,450**	−4	19,220	**20,020**	+4	117
Independent	13,250	**12,320**	−7	28,130	**27,050**	−4	36,620	**35,400**	−3	61
Other Denominations	10,910	**11,140**	+2	25,360	**25,610**	+1	35,510	**34,310**	−3	58
TOTAL Protestant	138,100	**134,380**	−3	381,890	**373,370**	−2	1,113,800	**1,062,440**	−5	108
Roman Catholic	71,050	**68,880**	−3	296,030	**286,990**	−3	816,100[3]	**814,400[3]**	0	474
TOTAL ALL Churches	209,150	**203,260**	−3	677,920	**660,360**	−3	1,929,900	**1,876,840**	−3	163

	Church Attenders[2]			Civil Population		
Age Group	Male	Female	Total	Male	Female	Total
	%	%	%	%	%	%
Under 15	11	14	25	11	10	21
15-19	2	3	5	5	4	9
20-29	3	6	9	7	8	15
30-44	5	10	15	9	10	19
45-64	9	15	24	11	11	22
65 or over	7	15	22	5	9	14
All ages	37	63	100	48	52	100

[1] Morning and evening congregations combined where both held excluding twicers
[2] This table is based on responses from 66% of all the churches in Scotland
[3] Total Catholic population including children
[4] Conservative Presbyterian adherents included with members

SCOTLAND: TOTAL

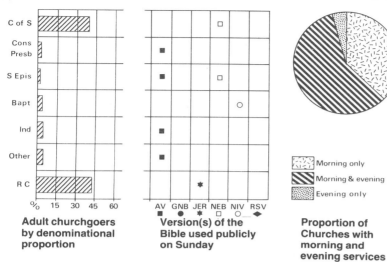

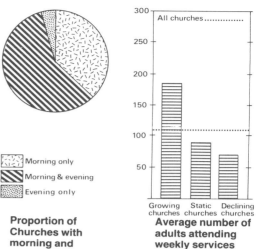

	Morning only
	Morning & evening
	Evening only

Adult churchgoers by denominational proportion

Version(s) of the Bible used publicly on Sunday

AV GNB JER NEB NIV RSV
■   ●   ✳   □   ○   ◆

Proportion of Churches with morning and evening services

Average number of adults attending weekly services

	Percentage of churches which between 1980 & 1984:			Version of the Bible most used:		1984 Adults attending twice on Sunday	1984 Churches whose Services were held:			Mid-week meetings 1984:	
	Grew	Remained Static	Declined	Sunday	Mid-week Meetings		Morning only	Morn. & Evening	Evening only	Churches with	Average attendance
	%	%	%			%	%	%	%	%	
Church of Scotland	29	41	30	NEB	GNB	11	59	40	1	53	16
Conservative Presbyterian	14	72	14	AV	AV	51	12	72	16	64	19
Scottish Episcopal	27	65	8	AV/NEB	GNB	11	59	38	3	54	12
Baptist	38	52	10	NIV	NIV	41	1	96	3	98	29
Independent	18	71	11	AV	AV	47	20	75	5	80	27
Other Denominations	26	65	9	AV	AV	34	28	62	10	67	17
All Protestant	27	52	21	AV	AV	19	46	50	4	61	19
Roman Catholic	20	56	24	JER	JER	3	25	73	2	45	32
All Churches	26	52	22	AV	AV	13	43	53	4	59	20

Number of adult attenders[2]	1984 Sizes of Sunday Congregations[1]								Average Congregation per Church[2]
	Under 10	10-25	26-50	51-100	101-150	151-200	201-300	Over 300	
	%	%	%	%	%	%	%	%	
All Protestant Churches	4	14	19	23	13	10	10	7	108
Growing Churches	2	4	6	22	15	14	19	18	182
Static Churches	5	17	26	19	13	9	8	3	90
Declining Churches	4	18	22	35	13	6	2	0	69
Roman Catholic Churches	2	4	4	9	8	4	9	60	474
Growing Churches	1	0	0	10	18	5	5	61	576
Static Churches	2	4	5	8	6	4	9	62	516
Declining Churches	1	7	6	10	3	5	16	52	392

[1] This table is based on responses from 73% of all the churches in Scotland
[2] Morning and evening services combined, where both held, excluding twicers.

BORDERS

Total Adult Population:	77,920
Change of adult population in four years:	+2%
Total child population (under 15):	19,300
Change of child population in four years:	−6%
Total number of churches:	144
Percentage of churches responding:	80%
Total number of ministers:	138
Percentage of churches holding mid-week meetings:	45%
1984 adult Protestant church membership as percentage of total adult population:	42%
1984 Roman Catholic church membership as percentage of total adult population:	5%
1984 adult church attenders (Protestant and Roman Catholic) as percentage of total adult population:	13%
1984 adult church adherents as percentage of total adult population:	3%

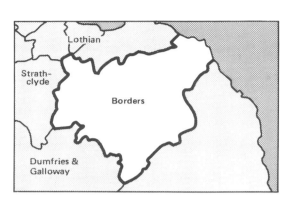

	Child Attenders			Adult Attenders			Membership			Average Sunday Congregation[1]
	1980	1984	Change	1980	1984	Change	1980	1984	Change	1984
			%			%			%	Adults
Church of Scotland	1,710	**1,810**	+6	6,810	**7,150**	+5	30,930	**29,480**	−5	74
Conservative Presbyterian	0	**0**	−	0	**0**	−	0	**0**	−	−
Scottish Episcopal	210	**230**	+10	510	**630**	+24	1,970	**1,690**	−14	53
Baptist	160	**140**	−13	300	**290**	−3	330	**310**	−6	42
Independent	170	**220**	+29	450	**620**	+38	950	**980**	+3	56
Other Denominations	70	**80**	+14	140	**130**	−7	220	**190**	−14	26
TOTAL Protestant	2,320	**2,480**	+7	8,210	**8,820**	+7	34,400	**32,650**	−5	67
Roman Catholic	330	**380**	+15	1,400	**1,580**	+13	3,720[3]	**4,130**[3]	+11	122
TOTAL All Churches	2,650	**2,860**	+8	9,610	**10,400**	+8	38,120	**36,780**	−4	72

	Church Attenders[2]			Civil Population		
Age Group	Male	Female	Total	Male	Female	Total
	%	%	%	%	%	%
Under 15	8	12	20	10	10	20
15-19	2	2	4	4	4	8
20-29	2	5	7	7	6	13
30-44	5	10	15	9	9	18
45-64	9	17	26	11	12	23
65 or over	10	18	28	7	11	18
ALL ages	36	64	100	48	52	100

[1] Morning and evening congregations combined where both held excluding twicers
[2] This table is based on responses from 66% of all the Protestant churches in Borders
[3] Total Catholic population including children

BORDERS

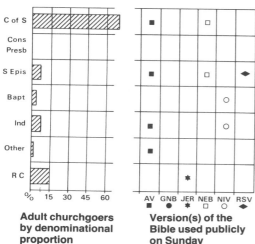

Adult churchgoers
by denominational
proportion

Version(s) of the
Bible used publicly
on Sunday

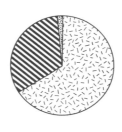

Proportion of
Churches with
morning and
evening services

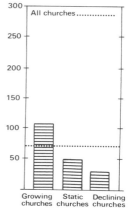

Average number of
adults attending
weekly services

	Percentage of churches which between 1980 & 1984:			Version of the Bible most used:		1984 Adults attending twice on Sunday	1984 Churches whose Services were held:			Mid-week meetings 1984:	
	Grew	Remained Static	Declined	Sunday	Mid-week Meetings		Morning only	Morn. & Evening	Evening only	Churches with	Average attendance
	%	%	%			%	%	%	%	%	
Church of Scotland	36	42	22	NEB/AV	NEB/RSV	8	75	25	0	32	11
Conservative Presbyterian	-	-	-	-	-	-	-	-	-	-	-
Scottish Episcopal[3]	25	75	0	Various	NEB	10	75	25	0	75	15
Baptist[3]	80	20	0	NIV	NIV	61	0	100	0	100	14
Independent[3]	50	50	0	AV/NIV	AV/NIV	42	25	62	13	87	20
Other Denominations[3]	17	83	0	AV	AV/GNB	43	17	83	0	83	10
All Protestant	38	45	17	AV/NIV	RSV	26	64	35	1	44	12
Roman Catholic	36	64	0	JER	JER	2	82	18	0	50	9
All Churches	37	47	16	AV	RSV	19	66	33	1	45	12

Number of adult attenders[2]	1984 Sizes of Sunday Congregations[1]								Average Congregation per Church[2]
	Under 10	10-25	26-50	51-100	101-150	151-200	201-300	Over 300	
	%	%	%	%	%	%	%	%	
All Protestant Churches	1	18	38	26	8	4	4	1	67
Growing Churches	0	8	21	33	15	10	10	3	107
Static Churches	2	15	51	26	6	0	0	0	48
Declining Churches	0	50	39	11	0	0	0	0	29
Roman Catholic Churches	0	0	18	27	18	28	0	9	122

[1] This table is based on responses from 80% of all the churches in Borders
[2] Where held, morning and evening services combined excluding twicers
[3] Percentages unreliable because based on a particularly small number of churches

CENTRAL

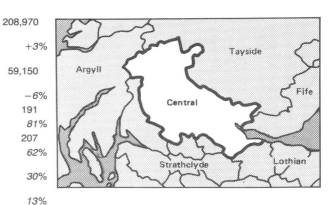

Total Adult Population:	208,970
Change of adult population in four years:	+3%
Total child population (under 15):	59,150
Change of child population in four years:	−6%
Total number of churches:	191
Percentage of churches responding:	81%
Total number of ministers:	207
Percentage of churches holding mid-week meetings:	62%
1984 adult Protestant church membership as percentage of total adult population:	30%
1984 Roman Catholic church membership as percentage of total adult population:	13%
1984 adult church attenders (Protestant and Roman Catholic) as percentage of total adult population:	14%
1984 adult church adherents as percentage of total adult population:	1%

	Child Attenders			Adult Attenders			Membership			Average Sunday Congregation[1]
	1980	1984	Change	1980	1984	Change	1980	1984	Change	1984
			%			%			%	Adults
Church of Scotland	4,960	**5,450**	+ 10	15,770	**15,300**	− 3	58,270	**55,700**	− 4	168
Conservative Presbyterian	10	**10**	0	30	**30**	0	30	**30**	0	33
Scottish Episcopal	170	**240**	+ 41	650	**930**	+ 43	1,690	**1,780**	+ 5	62
Baptist	430	**460**	+ 7	840	**980**	+ 17	910	**970**	+ 7	89
Independent	790	**660**	− 16	1,710	**1,590**	− 7	1,680	**1,530**	− 9	93
Other Denominations	590	**630**	+ 7	1,480	**1,520**	+ 3	2,960	**2,880**	− 3	63
TOTAL Protestant	6,950	**7,450**	+ 7	20,480	**20,350**	− 1	65,540	**62,890**	− 4	128
Roman Catholic	2,160	**2,210**	+ 2	9,000	**9,190**	+ 2	24,600[3]	**26,480**[3]	+ 8	287
TOTAL All Churches	9,110	**9,660**	+ 6	29,480	**29,540**	0	90,140	**89,370**	− 1	155

	Church Attenders[2]			Civil Population		
Age Group	Male	Female	Total	Male	Female	Total
	%	%	%	%	%	%
Under 15	11	13	24	11	11	22
15-19	3	3	6	5	4	9
20-29	3	6	9	7	7	14
30-44	6	11	17	10	10	20
45-64	8	16	24	11	11	22
65 or over	7	13	20	5	8	13
All ages	38	62	100	49	51	100

[1] Morning and evening congregations combined where both held excluding twicers
[2] This table is based on responses from 74% of all the Protestant churches in Central
[3] Total Catholic population including children

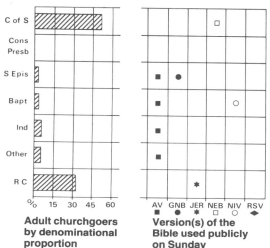

Adult churchgoers by denominational proportion

Version(s) of the Bible used publicly on Sunday

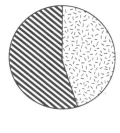

Morning only

Morning & evening

Evening only

Proportion of Churches with morning and evening services

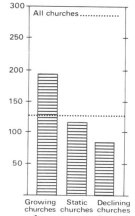

Average number of adults attending weekly services

	Percentage of churches which between 1980 & 1984:			Version of the Bible most used:		1984 Adults attending twice on Sunday	1984 Churches whose Services were held:			Mid-week meetings 1984:	
	Grew	Remained Static	Declined	Sunday	Mid-week Meetings		Morning only	Morn. & Evening	Evening only	Churches with	Average attendance
	%	%	%			%	%	%	%	%	
Church of Scotland	30	40	30	NEB	GNB	9	58	42	0	62	14
Conservative Presbyterian	–	–	–	–	–	–	–	–	–	–	–
Scottish Episcopal	17	83	0	AV/GNB	GNB	5	50	50	0	45	17
Baptist	50	40	10	AV/NIV	NIV	40	0	100	0	100	21
Independent[3]	0	100	0	AV	AV	49	29	71	0	100	21
Other Denominations	23	64	13	AV	GNB	29	32	68	0	68	14
All Protestant	28	51	21	AV	GNB	17	48	52	0	67	16
Roman Catholic	30	48	22	JER	JER	2	26	74	0	30	18
All Churches	28	50	22	AV	GNB	12	45	55	0	62	16

Number of adult attenders[2]	1984 Sizes of Sunday Congregations[1]								Average Congregation per Church[2]
	Under 10	10-25	26-50	51-100	101-150	151-200	201-300	Over 300	
	%	%	%	%	%	%	%	%	
All Protestant Churches	2	7	14	27	15	14	16	5	128
Growing Churches	0	5	3	16	8	19	41	8	192
Static Churches	3	9	21	18	18	18	9	4	115
Declining Churches	4	4	11	64	14	0	0	3	82
Roman Catholic Churches	0	9	9	9	4	4	17	48	287

[1] This table is based on responses from 81% of all the churches in Central
[2] Morning services and evening services combined excluding twicers
[3] Percentages unreliable because based on a particularly small number of churches

DUMFRIES AND GALLOWAY

Total Adult Population: 112,640

Change of adult population in four years: +2%

Total child population (under 15): 29,250

Change of child population in four years: − 8%

Total number of churches: 175

Percentage of churches responding: 73%

Total number of ministers: 156

Percentage of churches holding mid-week meetings: 43%

1984 adult Protestant church membership as percentage of total adult population: 41%

1984 Roman Catholic church membership as percentage of total adult population: 10%

1984 adult church attenders (Protestand and Roman Catholic) as percentage of total adult population: 14%

1984 adult church adherents as percentage of total adult population: 2%

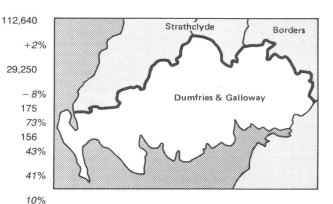

	Child Attenders			Adult Attenders			Membership			Average Sunday Congregation[1]
	1980	1984	Change	1980	1984	Change	1980	1984	Change	1984
			%			%			%	Adults
Church of Scotland	3,520	3,140	− 11	9,600	10,340	+8	44,390	42,770	− 4	99
Conservative Presbyterian	20	20	0	90	80	− 11	220	210	− 5	39
Scottish Episcopal	120	140	+17	620	690	+11	1,810	1,700	− 6	41
Baptist	110	130	+18	270	270	0	130	150	+15	91
Independent	470	450	− 4	850	870	+2	1,110	1,160	+5	41
Other Denominations	80	60	− 25	200	220	+10	400	370	− 7	25
TOTAL Protestant	4,320	3,940	− 9	11,630	12,470	+7	48,060	46,360	− 4	80
Roman Catholic	860	760	− 8	3,450	3,170	− 8	12,210[3]	11,090[3]	− 9	167
TOTAL All Churches	5,150	4,700	− 9	15,080	15,640	+4	60,270	57,450	− 5	89

Age Group	Church Attenders[2]			Civil Population		
	Male	Female	Total	Male	Female	Total
	%	%	%	%	%	%
Under 15	10	13	23	11	10	21
15-19	2	3	5	5	4	9
20-29	3	4	7	7	6	13
30-44	5	9	14	9	9	18
45-64	11	16	27	11	12	23
65 or over	8	16	24	6	10	16
All ages	39	61	100	49	51	100

[1] Morning and evening congregations combined where both held excluding twicers
[2] This table is based on responses from 66% of all the Protestant churches in Dumfries and Galloway
[3] Total Catholic population including children

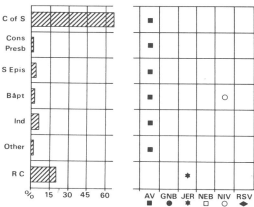

Adult churchgoers by denominational proportion

Version(s) of the Bible used publicly on Sunday

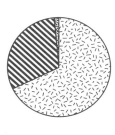

Morning only

Morning & evening

Evening only

Proportion of Churches with morning and evening services

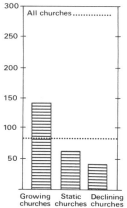

Average number of adults attending weekly services

	Percentage of churches which between 1980 & 1984:			Version of the Bible most used:		1984 Adults attending twice on Sunday	1984 Churches whose Services were held:			Mid-week meetings 1984:	
	Grew	Remained Static	Declined	Sunday	Mid-week Meetings		Morning only	Morn. & Evening	Evening only	Churches with	Average attendance
	%	%	%			%	%	%	%	%	
Church of Scotland	27	44	29	AV	GN	10	79	21	0	41	13
Conservative Presbyterian[3]	0	100	0	AV	AV	18	0	100	0	100	12
Scottish Episcopal	31	69	0	AV	GNB/RSV	4	77	23	0	42	17
Baptist[3]	33	67	0	AV/ NIV	NIV	39	0	100	0	100	18
Independent[3]	0	100	0	AV	AV	49	17	83	0	83	15
Other Denominations[3]	50	50	0	AV	AV	35	25	62	13	38	10
All Protestant	27	51	22	AV	AV	16	69	30	1	45	14
Roman Catholic	18	64	18	JER	JER	3	55	45	0	25	11
All Churches	27	52	21	AV	AV	13	68	31	1	43	14

Number of adult attenders[2]	1984 Sizes of Sunday Congregations[1]								Average Congregation per Church[2]
	Under 10	10-25	26-50	51-100	101-150	151-200	201-300	Over 300	
	%	%	%	%	%	%	%	%	
All Protestant Churches	2	23	28	19	12	10	4	2	80
Growing Churches	0	19	0	19	21	19	16	6	140
Static Churches	2	22	38	18	10	10	0	0	61
Declining Churches	4	32	40	20	4	0	0	0	39
Roman Catholic Churches	0	9	18	9	28	9	18	9	167

[1] This table is based on responses from 73% of all the churches in Dumfries and Galloway
[2] Where held morning and evening services combined excluding twicers
[3] Percentage unreliable because based on a particularly small number of churches

FIFE

Total Adult Population:	254,720
Change of adult population in four years:	+2%
Total child population (under 15):	70,350
Change of child population in four years:	−7%
Total number of churches:	250
Percentage of churches responding:	71%
Total number of ministers:	228
Percentage of churches holding mid-week meetings:	59%
1984 adult Protestant church membership as percentage of total adult population:	28%
1984 Roman Catholic church membership as percentage of total adult population	9%
1984 adult church attenders (Protestant and Roman Catholic) as percentage of total adult population:	12%
1984 adult church adherents as percentage of total adult population:	1%

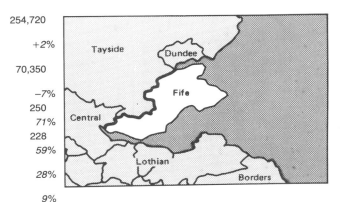

	Child Attenders			Adult Attenders			Membership			Average Sunday Congregation[1]
	1980	1984	Change	1980	1984	Change	1980	1984	Change	1984
			%			%			%	Adults
Church of Scotland	5,580	5,810	+4	14,410	15,450	+7	66,590	62,060	−7	140
Conservative Presbyterian	20	30	†	60	60	0	80	70	−12	19
Scottish Episcopal	280	340	+21	1,150	1,280	+11	2,610	2,610	0	67
Baptist	700	540	−23	2,340	1,830	−22	1,800	1,910	+6	112
Independent	470	530	+13	1,680	1,660	−1	2,380	2,560	+8	52
Other Denominations	530	700	+32	1,470	1,660	+13	2,320	2,270	−2	48
TOTAL Protestant	7,580	7,950	+5	21,110	21,940	+4	75,780	71,480	−6	102
Roman Catholic	2,340	2,130	−9	9,730	8,890	−9	23,700[3]	23,650[3]	0	278
TOTAL All Churches	9,920	10,080	+2	30,840	30,830	0	99,480	95,130	−4	123

	Church Attenders[2]			Civil Population		
Age Group	Male	Female	Total	Male	Female	Total
	%	%	%	%	%	%
Under 15	10	15	25	11	11	22
15–19	2	4	6	5	4	9
20–29	3	5	8	7	7	14
30–44	5	10	15	9	10	19
45–64	8	15	23	11	11	22
65 or over	7	16	23	6	8	14
All ages	35	65	100	49	51	100

[1] Morning and evening congregations combined where both held excluding twicers
[2] This table is based on responses from 59% of all the churches in Fife
[3] Total Catholic population including children
†Numbers too small to give a meaningful percentage

FIFE

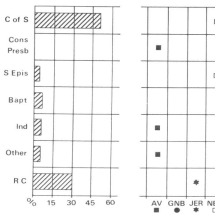

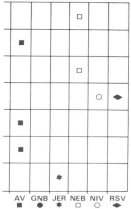

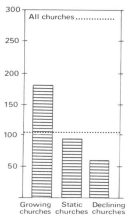

| **Adult churchgoers by denominational proportion** | **Version(s) of the Bible used publicly on Sunday** | **Proportion of Churches with morning and evening services** | **Average number of adults attending weekly services** |

| Morning only |
| Morning & evening |
| Evening only |

	Percentage of churches which between 1980 & 1984:			Version of the Bible most used:		1984 Adults attending twice on Sunday	1984 Churches whose Services were held:			Mid-week meetings 1984:	
	Grew	Remained Static	Declined	Sunday	Mid-week Meetings		Morning only	Morn. & Evening	Evening only	Churches with	Average attendance
	%	%	%			%	%	%	%	%	
Church of Scotland	32	43	25	NEB	GNB	8	65	35	0	48	15
Conservative Presbyterian[3]	0	100	0	AV	AV	27	33	67	0	100	10
Scottish Episcopal[3]	33	56	11	NEB	NEB	4	56	44	0	71	13
Baptist	15	54	31	NIV/RSV	AV	41	0	100	0	100	26
Independent	31	50	19	AV	AV/NIV	33	38	56	6	75	26
Other Denominations	15	81	4	AV	AV/GNB	43	38	54	8	62	21
All Protestant	27	53	20	AV	GNB/AV	20	51	47	2	60	19
Roman Catholic	9	70	21	JER	JER	1	26	74	0	48	11
All Churches	25	55	20	AV	GNB	13	48	50	2	59	18

Number of adult attenders[2]	1984 Sizes of Sunday Congregations[1]								Average Congregation per Church[2]
	Under 10	10-25	26-50	51-100	101-150	151-200	201-300	Over 300	
	%	%	%	%	%	%	%	%	
All Protestant Churches	4	11	19	22	18	14	8	4	102
Growing Churches	0	7	7	12	10	28	26	10	179
Static Churches	6	12	23	14	30	11	1	3	92
Declining Churches	3	13	23	58	0	3	0	0	59
Roman Catholic Churches	0	0	4	0	13	9	13	61	278

[1] This table is based on responses from 71% of all the churches in Fife
[2] Where held morning and evening services combined excluding twicers
[3] Percentage unreliable because based on a particularly small number of churches

GRAMPIAN: ABERDEEN

Total Adult Population:	162,640
Change of adult population in four years:	0%
Total child population (under 15):	37,190
Change of child population in four years:	−10%
Total number of churches:	109
Percentage of churches responding:	72%
Total number of ministers:	93
Percentage of churches holding mid-week meetings:	59%
1984 adult Protestant church membership as percentage of total adult population:	29%
1984 Roman Catholic church membership as percentage of total adult population:	3%
1984 adult church attenders (Protestant and Roman Catholic) as percentage of total adult population:	9%
1984 adult church adherents as percentage of total adult population:	1%

	Child Attenders			Adult Attenders			Membership			Average Sunday Congregation[1]
	1980	1984	Change	1980	1984	Change	1980	1984	Change	1984
			%			%			%	Adults
Church of Scotland	3,570	2,900	−19	11,000	9,770	−11	43,860	42,520	−3	181
Conservative Presbyterian	60	80	+33	190	190	0	350	370	+6	96
Scottish Episcopal	60	90	+50	270	360	+33	1,120	1,200	+7	33
Baptist	180	210	+17	760	950	+25	760	820	+8	190
Independent	500	620	+24	1,070	1,310	+22	1,390	1,650	+19	93
Other Denominations	280	250	−11	180	620	+29	690	720	+4	44
TOTAL Protestant	4,650	4,150	−11	13,770	13,200	−4	48,170	47,280	−2	132
Roman Catholic	520	480	−8	2,190	1,990	−9	3,370[3]	4,640[3]	+38	221
TOTAL All Churches	5,170	4,630	−10	15,960	15,190	−5	51,540	51,920	+1	139

	Church Attenders[2]			Civil Population		
Age Group	Male	Female	Total	Male	Female	Total
	%	%	%	%	%	%
Under 15	10	12	22	10	9	19
15–19	3	4	7	4	5	9
20–29	4	7	11	8	8	16
30–44	6	10	16	9	9	18
45–64	8	15	23	11	12	23
65 or over	7	14	21	6	9	15
All ages	38	62	100	48	52	100

[1] Morning and evening congregations combined where both held excluding twicers
[2] This table is based on responses from 66% of all the Protestant churches in Aberdeen
[3] Total Catholic population including children

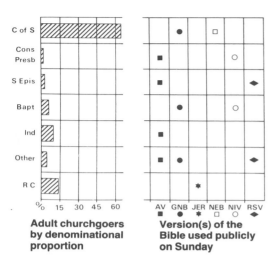

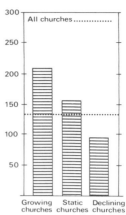

Morning only

Morning & evening

Evening only

Adult churchgoers by denominational proportion

Version(s) of the Bible used publicly on Sunday

AV GNB JER NEB NIV RSV
■ ● ✳ □ ○ ◆

Proportion of Churches with morning and evening services

Average number of adults attending weekly services

Growing churches Static churches Declining churches

	Percentage of churches which between 1980 & 1984:			Version of the Bible most used:		1984 Adults attending twice on Sunday	1984 Churches whose Services were held:			Mid-week meetings 1984:	
	Grew	Remained Static	Declined	Sunday	Mid-week Meetings		Morning only	Morn. & Evening	Evening only	Churches with	Average attendance
	%	%	%			%	%	%	%	%	
Church of Scotland	25	34	41	GNB/NEB	GNB	14	43	57	0	53	21
Conservative Presbyterian	0	100	0	AV/NIV	AV/NIV	52	0	100	0	100	33
Scottish Episcopal[3]	33	67	0	AV/RSV	–	✳	100	0	0	0	–
Baptist[3]	50	50	0	NIV/GNB	NIV	40	0	100	0	100	42
Independent[3]	33	56	11	AV	AV	34	33	56	11	89	38
Other Denominations[3]	29	57	14	Various	GNB	26	29	57	14	71	13
All Protestant	28	43	29	GNB	GNB	22	39	58	3	61	26
Roman Catholic[3]	42	29	29	JER	JER	2	37	50	13	38	26
All Churches	29	42	29	GNB	GNB	18	39	57	4	59	26

	1984 Sizes of Sunday Congregations[1]								Average Congregation per Church[2]
Number of adult attenders[2]	Under 10	10-25	26-50	51-100	101-150	151-200	201-300	Over 300	
	%	%	%	%	%	%	%	%	
All Protestant Churches	1	3	10	25	23	12	16	10	132
Growing Churches	0	0	5	21	5	16	37	16	208
Static Churches	0	7	17	13	24	13	13	13	154
Declining Churches	5	0	5	45	40	5	0	0	95
Roman Catholic Churches	0	0	0	0	57	0	14	29	221

[1] This table is based on responses from 70% of all the churches in Aberdeen
[2] Where held, morning and evening services combined excluding twicers
[3] Percentages unreliable because based on a particularly small number of churches

GRAMPIAN: OTHER

Total Adult Population:	201,970
Change of adult population in four years:	+7%
Total child population (under 15):	61,100
Change of child population in four years:	+3%
Total number of churches:	298
Percentage of churches responding:	68%
Total number of ministers:	252
Percentage of churches holding mid-week meetings:	44%
1984 adult Protestant church membership as percentage of total adult population:	44%
1984 adult Roman Catholic church membership as percentage of total adult population:	3%
1984 adult church attenders (Protestant and Roman Catholic) as percentage of total adult population:	14%
1984 adult church adherents as percentage of total adult population:	4%

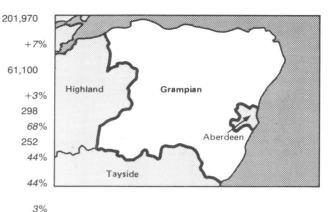

	Child Attenders			Adult Attenders			Membership			Average Sunday Congregation[1]
	1980	1984	Change	1980	1984	Change	1980	1984	Change	1984
			%			%			%	Adults
Church of Scotland	7,780	7,910	+2	17,780	18,100	+2	82,160	82,980	+1	112
Conservative Presbyterian	20	20	0	100	90	−10	130	130	0	22
Scottish Episcopal	280	430	+54	1,100	1,440	+31	3,400	3,390	0	32
Baptist	600	740	+23	980	1,220	+24	640	740	+16	186
Independent	640	590	−8	1,440	1,720	+19	620	850	+37	56
Other Denominations	1,080	1,000	−7	2,090	2,040	−2	1,570	1,160	−26	68
TOTAL Protestant	10,400	10,690	+3	23,490	24,610	+5	88,520	89,250	+1	89
Roman Catholic	690	730	+6	2,880	3,060	+6	5,110[3]	5,980[3]	+17	133
TOTAL All Churches	11,090	11,420	+3	26,370	27,670	+5	93,630	95,230	+2	93

Age Group	Church Attenders[2]			Civil Population		
	Male	Female	Total	Male	Female	Total
	%	%	%	%	%	%
Under 15	13	18	31	12	11	23
15-19	2	4	6	4	4	8
20-29	3	5	8	7	7	14
30-44	6	9	15	11	10	21
45-64	8	13	21	10	10	20
65 or over	7	12	19	6	8	14
All ages	39	61	100	50	50	100

[1] Morning and evening congregations combined where both held excluding twicers
[2] This table is based on responses from 62% of all the Protestant churches in Grampian other than Aberdeen
[3] Total Catholic population including children

GRAMPIAN: OTHER

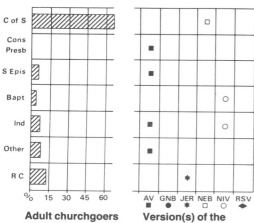

Adult churchgoers by denominational proportion

Version(s) of the Bible used publicly on Sunday

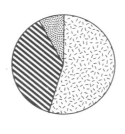

Morning only
Morning & evening
Evening only

Proportion of Churches with morning and evening services

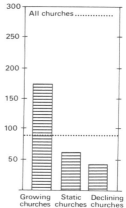

Average number of adults attending weekly services

	Percentage of churches which between 1980 & 1984:			Version of the Bible most used:		1984 Adults attending twice on Sunday	1984 Churches whose Services were held:			Mid-week meetings 1984:	
	Grew	Remained Static	Declined	Sunday	Mid-week Meetings		Morning only	Morn. & Evening	Evening only	Churches with	Average attendance
	%	%	%			%	%	%	%	%	
Church of Scotland	33	32	35	NEB	GNB	11	66	32	2	38	14
Conservative Presbyterian[3]	0	100	0	AV	AV	36	0	67	33	67	13
Scottish Episcopal	21	74	5	AV	GNB/NEB	10	68	27	5	37	11
Baptist[3]	100	0	0	NIV	NIV	41	0	100	0	100	31
Independent	33	42	25	AV/NIV	AV/NIV	25	25	50	25	75	16
Other Denominations	23	64	13	AV	AV	40	27	59	14	50	34
All Protestant	32	41	27	AV	GNB	19	56	38	6	44	17
Roman Catholic	33	61	6	JER	JER	2	27	46	27	44	12
All Churches	32	42	26	AV	GNB	17	54	38	8	44	17

	1984 Sizes of Sunday Congregations[1]								Average Congregation per Church[2]
Number of adult attenders[2]	Under 10	10-25	26-50	51-100	101-150	151-200	201-300	Over 300	
	%	%	%	%	%	%	%	%	
All Protestant Churches	8	16	21	22	12	9	8	4	89
Growing Churches	2	3	5	14	20	24	22	10	175
Static Churches	16	19	23	22	13	3	3	1	61
Declining Churches	4	28	36	30	0	2	0	0	43
Roman Catholic Churches	0	7	7	20	20	7	26	13	133

[1] This table is based on responses from 67% of all the churches in Grampian other than Aberdeen
[2] Where held, morning and evening services combined excluding twicers
[3] Percentages unreliable because based on a particularly small number of churches

HIGHLAND [1]

Total Adult population: 186,860

Change of adult population
in four years: +17%

Total child population
(under 15): 53,880

Change of child population
in four years: +11%

Total number of churches: 485

Percentage of churches
responding: 74%

Total number of ministers: 399

Percentage of churches holding mid-week meetings: 59%

1984 adult Protestant church membership as
percentage of total adult population: 24%

1984 Roman Catholic church membership as
percentage of total adult population: 7%

1984 adult church attenders (Protestant and
Roman Catholic) as percentage of total adult population: 18%

1984 adult church adherents as percentage of
total adult population: 9%

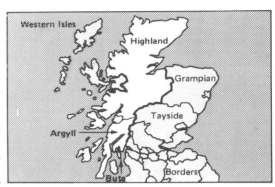

	Child Attenders			Adult Attenders			Membership			Average Sunday Congregation [5]
	1980	1984	Change	1980	1984	Change	1980	1984	Change	1984
			%			%			%	Adults
Church of Scotland	5,660	**6,150**	+9	16,700	**17,680**	+6	33,030	**32,330**	−2	98
Conservative Presbyterian	930	**1,050**	+13	4,880	**4,520**	−7	6,490[4]	**6,670**[4]	+3	35
Scottish Episcopal	280	**340**	+21	1,220	**1,340**	+10	3,050	**2,870**	−6	33
Baptist	240	**350**	+46	860	**960**	+12	520	**630**	+21	57
Independent	320	**300**	−6	920	**820**	−11	820	**880**	+7	43
Other Denominations	530	**490**	−8	970	**1,110**	+14	1,040	**1,150**	+11	53
TOTAL Protestant	7,960	**8,680**	+9	25,550	**26,400**	+3	44,950	**44,530**	−1	65
Roman Catholic	1,580	**1,620**	+3	6,600	**6,770**	+3	12,550[3]	**13,970**[3]	+11	89
TOTAL All Churches	9,540	**10,300**	+8	32,150	**33,170**	+3	57,500	**58,500**	+2	68

	Church Attenders[2]			Civil Population		
Age Group	Male	Female	Total	Male	Female	Total
	%	%	%	%	%	%
Under 15	10	13	23	11	11	22
15-19	2	3	5	5	4	9
20-29	3	4	7	7	7	14
30-44	6	10	16	10	9	19
45-64	9	15	24	10	11	21
65 or over	9	16	25	6	9	15
All ages	39	61	100	49	51	100

[1] Excluding Skye and Lochalsh but including Argyll and Bute
[2] This table is based on responses from 69% of all the Protestant churches in Highland
[3] Total Catholic population including children
[4] Conservative Presbyterian adherents included with membership
[5] Morning and evening congregations combined where both held excluding twicers

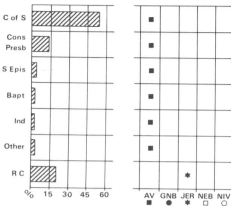

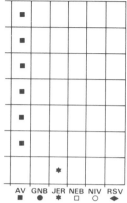

Morning only

Morning & evening

Evening only

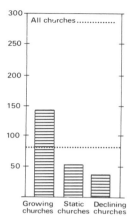

Adult churchgoers by denominational proportion

Version(s) of the Bible used publicly on Sunday

Proportion of Churches with morning and evening services

Adult churchgoers by denominational proportion

	Percentage of churches which between 1980 & 1984:			Version of the Bible most used:		1984 Adults attending twice on Sunday	1984 Churches whose Services were held:			Mid-week meetings 1984:	
	Grew	Remained Static	Declined	Sunday	Mid-week Meetings		Morning only	Morn. & Evening	Evening only	Churches with	Average attendance
	%	%	%			%	%	%	%	%	
Church of Scotland	25	44	31	AV	GNB	12	53	45	2	62	12
Conservative Presbyterian	13	76	11	AV	AV	53	15	69	16	57	17
Scottish Episcopal	29	65	6	AV	AV/NEB	13	62	29	9	38	9
Baptist	30	70	0	AV	AV	56	0	90	10	91	20
Independent[4]	17	66	17	AV	AV	55	17	83	0	100	24
Other Denominations	22	67	11	AV	AV	38	22	72	6	67	13
All Protestant	22	58	20	AV	AV	25	39	54	7	60	14
Roman Catholic	23	54	23	JER	JER	12	57	34	9	49	19
All Churches	22	57	21	AV	AV	23	41	52	7	59	14

Number of adult attenders [3]	1984 Sizes of Sunday Congregations[2]								Average Congregation per Church [3]
	Under 10	10-25	26-50	51-100	101-150	151-200	201-300	Over 300	
	%	%	%	%	%	%	%	%	
All Protestant Churches	9	24	23	28	6	4	3	3	65
Growing Churches	4	7	3	33	19	12	12	10	142
Static Churches	11	26	28	25	4	3	2	1	52
Declining Churches	6	38	28	28	0	0	0	0	37
Roman Catholic Churches	14	17	11	17	14	9	9	9	89

[1] Excluding Skye and Lochalsh but including Argyll and Bute
[2] This table is based on responses from 73% of all the churches in Highland
[3] Where held morning and evening services combined excluding twicers
[4] Percentage unreliable because based on a particularly small number of churches

LOTHIAN: EDINBURGH

Total Adult Population:	350,010
Change of adult population in four years:	−2%
Total child population (under 15):	75,250
Change of child population in four years:	−13%
Total number of churches:	232
Percentage of Churches responding:	78%
Total number of ministers:	244
Percentage of churches holding mid-week meetings:	67%
1984 adult Protestant church membership as percentage of total adult population:	25%
1984 Roman Catholic church membership as percentage of total adult population:	10%
1984 adult church attenders (Protestant and Roman Catholic) as percentage of total adult population:	12%
1984 adult church adherents as percentage of total adult population:	1%

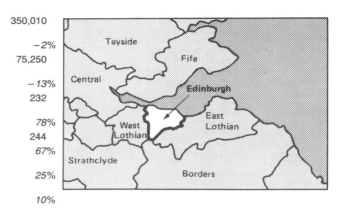

	Child Attenders			Adult Attenders			Membership			Average Sunday Congregation[1]
	1980	1984	Change	1980	1984	Change	1980	1984	Change	1984
			%			%			%	Adults
Church of Scotland	6,680	**6,000**	−10	21,050	**19,830**	−6	77,200	**72,010**	−7	202
Conservative Presbyterian	80	**80**	0	380	**410**	+8	680	**740**	+9	103
Scottish Episcopal	500	**540**	+8	2,190	**2,480**	+13	5,650	**5,670**	0	86
Baptist	870	**830**	−5	4,150	**3,580**	−14	3,500	**3,670**	+5	188
Independent	400	**350**	−13	1,210	**1,250**	+3	2,350	**2,070**	−12	73
Other Denominations	920	**800**	−13	2,280	**2,380**	+4	3,630	**3,310**	−9	68
TOTAL Protestant	9,450	**8,600**	−9	31,260	**29,930**	−4	93,010	**87,4,70**	−6	149
Roman Catholic	3,410	**2,910**	−15	14,230	**12,110**	−15	42,010[3]	**36,620**[3]	−13	391
TOTAL All Churches	12,860	**11,510**	-10	45,490	**42,040**	−8	135,020	**124,090**	−8	181

	Church Attenders[2]			Civil Population		
Age Group	Male	Female	Total	Male	Female	Total
	%	%	%	%	%	%
Under 15	7	11	18	9	9	18
15-19	2	3	5	4	4	8
20-29	5	7	12	8	8	16
30-44	6	10	16	9	9	18
45-64	8	15	23	11	12	23
65 or over	8	18	26	6	11	17
All ages	36	64	100	47	53	100

[1] Morning and evening congregations combined where both held excluding twicers
[2] This table is based on responses from 66% of all the Protestant churches in Edinburgh
[3] Total Catholic population including children

LOTHIAN: EDINBURGH

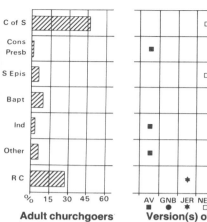

Adult churchgoers by denominational proportion

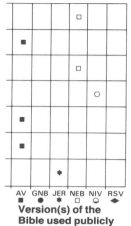

Version(s) of the Bible used publicly on Sunday

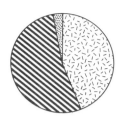

Proportion of Churches with morning and evening services

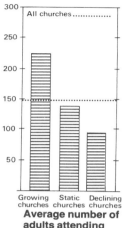

Average number of adults attending weekly services

	Percentage of churches which between 1980 & 1984:			Version of the Bible most used:		1984 Adults attending twice on Sunday	1984 Churches whose Services were held:			Mid-week meetings 1984:	
	Grew	Remained Static	Declined	Sunday	Mid-week Meetings		Morning only	Morn. & Evening	Evening only	Churches with	Average attendance
	%	%	%			%	%	%	%	%	
Church of Scotland	29	43	28	NEB	NEB	10	53	47	0	64	20
Conservative Presbyterian	*	*	*	AV	AV	79	0	100	0	100	55
Scottish Episcopal	38	57	5	NEB	NEB	11	52	48	0	71	17
Baptist	18	64	18	NIV	NIV/AV	41	9	91	0	100	41
Independent	18	73	9	AV	AV	32	45	46	9	73	38
Other Denominations	26	67	7	AV	AV	36	37	48	15	67	19
All Protestant	28	54	18	NEB	AV	23	46	51	3	69	23
Roman Catholic	21	38	42	JER	JER	2	29	67	4	54	19
All Churches	27	51	22	NEB	AV	16	44	53	3	67	23

Number of adult attenders[2]	1984 Sizes of Sunday Congregations[1]								Average Congregation per Church[2]
	Under 10	10-25	26-50	51-100	101-150	151-200	201-300	Over 300	
	%	%	%	%	%	%	%	%	
All Protestant Churches	1	7	12	22	19	9	18	12	149
Growing Churches	0	0	5	21	19	7	16	32	222
Static Churches	1	11	19	15	14	11	23	6	138
Declining Churches	4	7	3	45	31	7	3	0	94
Roman Catholic Churches	4	0	4	4	8	0	17	63	391

[1] This table is based on responses from 77% of all the churches in Edinburgh
[2] Morning and evening services combined when both held excluding twicers
* Too few churches to give a meaningful figure

LOTHIAN: OTHER

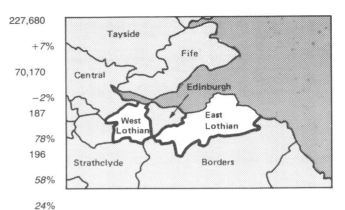

Total Adult Population:	227,680
Change of adult population in four years:	+7%
Total child population (under 15):	70,170
Change of child population in four years	−2%
Total number of churches:	187
Percentage of churches responding:	78%
Total number of ministers:	196
Percentage of churches holding mid-week meetings:	58%
1984 adult Protestant church membership as percentage of total adult population:	24%
1984 Roman Catholic church membership as percentage of total adult population:	15%
1984 adult church attenders (Protestant and Roman Catholic) as percentage of total adult population:	12%
1984 adult church adherents as percentage of total adult population:	2%

	Child Attenders			Adult Attenders			Membership			Average Sunday Congregation[1]
	1980	1984	Change	1980	1984	Change	1980	1984	Change	1984
			%			%			%	Adults
Church of Scotland	5,480	**4,990**	−9	12,140	**11,370**	−6	50,130	**46,960**	−6	131
Conservative Presbyterian	20	**40**	†	20	**60**	†	30	**80**	†	28
Scottish Episcopal	170	**210**	+23	610	**700**	+15	1,860	**1,880**	+1	50
Baptist	320	**350**	+9	690	**820**	+19	610	**740**	+21	117
Independent	460	**480**	+4	740	**790**	+7	1,050	**1,020**	−3	49
Other Denominations	1,050	**1,140**	+9	1,260	**1,550**	+23	3,020	**3,130**	+4	57
TOTAL Protestant	7,500	**7,210**	−4	15,460	**15,290**	−1	56,700	**53,810**	−5	100
Roman Catholic	6,630	**3,130**	−14	15,140	**13,040**	−14	39,760[3]	**34,600[3]**	−13	384
TOTAL All Churches	11,130	**10,340**	−7	30,600	**28,330**	−7	96,460	**88,410**	−8	151

	Church Attenders[2]			Civil Population		
Age Group	Male	Female	Total	Male	Female	Total
	%	%	%	%	%	%
Under 15	12	17	29	12	11	23
15-19	2	3	5	5	4	9
20-29	2	6	8	7	8	15
30-44	5	9	14	10	11	21
45-64	8	15	23	10	11	21
65 or over	7	14	21	5	6	11
All ages	36	64	100	49	51	100

[1] Morning and evening congregatiions combined where both held excluding twicers
[2] This table is based on responses from 67% of all the Protestant churches in Lothian, other than Edinburgh
[3] Total Catholic population including children
†Numbers too small to give a meaningful percentage

LOTHIAN: OTHER

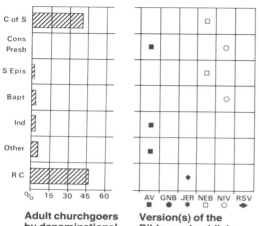

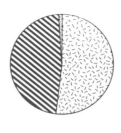

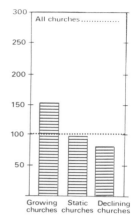

Adult churchgoers by denominational proportion

Version(s) of the Bible used publicly on Sunday

AV ■ GNB ● JER ✱ NEB □ NIV ○ RSV ◆

Proportion of Churches with morning and evening services

Morning only
Morning & evening
Evening only

Average number of adults attending weekly services

	Percentage of churches which between 1980 & 1984:			Version of the Bible most used:		1984 Adults attending twice on Sunday	1984 Churches whose Services were held:			Mid-week meetings 1984:	
	Grew	Remained Static	Declined	Sunday	Mid-week Meetings		Morning only	Morn. & Evening	Evening only	Churches with	Average attendance
	%	%	%			%	%	%	%	%	
Church of Scotland	29	40	31	NEB	GNB	10	66	33	1	57	12
Conservative Presbyterian	*	*	*	AV/NIV	AV/NIV	50	0	100	0	100	14
Scottish Episcopal[3]	40	60	0	NEB	NEB	*	80	20	0	100	15
Baptist[3]	50	50	0	NIV	NIV	35	0	100	0	100	31
Independent[3]	17	83	0	AV	AV	28	33	67	0	83	15
Other Denominations	47	47	6	AV	AV	48	32	68	0	75	14
All Protestant	33	45	22	AV	GNB	29	55	44	1	66	14
Roman Catholic	12	71	17	JER	JER	2	44	56	0	34	33
TOTAL All Churches	28	51	21	AV	GNB	13	52	47	1	58	17

Number of adult attenders[2]	1984 Sizes of Sunday Congregations[1]								Average Congregation per Church[2]
	Under 10	10-25	26-50	51-100	101-150	151-200	201-300	Over 300	
	%	%	%	%	%	%	%	%	
All Protestant Churches	0	15	19	25	15	13	10	3	100
Growing Churches	0	3	8	43	8	8	19	11	151
Static Churches	0	22	23	4	23	22	6	0	97
Declining Churches	0	17	29	42	8	0	4	0	64
Roman Catholic Churches	0	3	3	12	3	0	12	67	384

[1] This table is based on responses from 76% of all the churches in Lothian, other than Edinburgh
[2] Morning and evening services combined where both held excluding twicers
[3] Percentage unreliable because based on a particularly small number of churches
* Too few churches to give a meaningful figure

ORKNEY ISLANDS

Total Adult Population	14,400
Change of adult population in four years	+4%
Total child population (under 15):	3,990
Change of child population in four years:	0%
Total number of churches:	45
Percentage of churches responding:	69%
Total number of ministers:	33
Percentage of churches holding mid-week meetings:	52%
1984 adult Protestant church membership as percentage of total adult population:	45%
1984 Roman Catholic church membership as percentage of total adult population:	1%
1984 adult church attenders (Protestant and Roman Catholic) as percentage of total adult population:	14%
1984 adult church adherents as percentage of total adult population:	3%

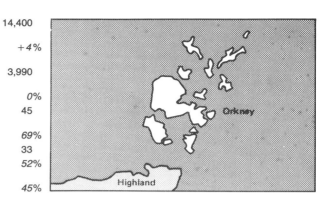

	Child Attenders			Adult Attenders			Membership			Average Sunday Congregation[1]
	1980	1984	Change	1980	1984	Change	1980	1984	Change	1984
			%			%			%	Adults
Church of Scotland	570	**490**	−14	1,350	**1,390**	+3	5,510	**5,160**	−6	50
Conservative Presbyterian	0	**0**	−	0	**0**	−	0	**0**	−	−
Scottish Episcopal	20	**20**	0	80	**90**	+13	260	**260**	0	43
Baptist	80	**70**	−13	150	**150**	0	120	**130**	+8	73
Independent	120	**120**	0	290	**260**	−10	490	**470**	−4	29
Other Denominations	60	**60**	0	130	**120**	−8	140	**150**	+7	41
TOTAL Protestant	850	**760**	−11	2,000	**2,010**	+1	6,520	**6,170**	−5	45
Roman Catholic	10	**10**	0	60	**60**	0	180[3]	**180[3]**	0	60
TOTAL All Churches	860	**770**	−10	**2,060**	2,070	0	6,700	**6,350**	−5	46

	Church Attenders[2]			Civil Population		
Age Group	Male	Female	Total	Male	Female	Total
	%	%	%	%	%	%
Under 15	9	17	26	11	11	22
15-19	3	2	5	4	4	8
20-29	3	4	7	6	6	12
30-44	6	9	15	10	10	20
45-64	9	15	24	10	11	21
65 or over	9	14	23	8	9	17
All ages	39	61	100	49	51	100

[1] Morning and evening congregations combined where both held excluding twicers
[2] This table is based on responses from 68% of all the Protestant churches in Orkney
[3] Total Catholic population including children

ORKNEY ISLANDS

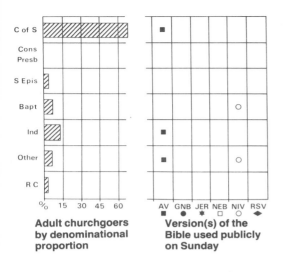

Adult churchgoers by denominational proportion

Version(s) of the Bible used publicly on Sunday

Morning only

Morning & evening

Evening only

Proportion of Churches with morning and evening services

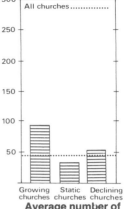

Average number of adults attending weekly services

	Percentage of churches which between 1980 & 1984:			Version of the Bible most used:		1984 Adults attending twice on Sunday	1984 Churches whose Services were held:			Mid-week meetings 1984:	
	Grew	Remained Static	Declined	Sunday	Mid-week Meetings		Morning only	Morn. & Evening	Evening only	Churches with	Average attendance
	%	%	%			%	%	%	%	%	
Church of Scotland	23	64	13	AV	AV	16	68	27	5	39	17
Conservative Presbyterian	–	–	–	–		–	–	–	–	–	–
Scottish Episcopal	*	*	*	*	*	*	0	100	0	*	*
Baptist	*	*	*	NIV	NIV	59	0	100	0	100	25
Independent[3]	0	100	0	AV	AV	61	0	100	0	80	17
Other Denominations	*	*	*	AV/NIV	AV/NIV	58	0	100	0	100	13
All Protestant	23	67	10	AV	AV	32	50	47	3	52	17
Roman Catholic	*	*	*	*	*	*	0	100	0	*	*
All Churches	23	67	10	AV	AV	32	50	47	3	52	17

	1984 Sizes of Sunday Congregations[1]								Average Congregation per Church[2]
Number of adult attenders[2]	Under 10	10-25	26-50	51-100	101-150	151-200	201-300	Over 300	
	%	%	%	%	%	%	%	%	
All Protestant Churches	3	30	37	24	0	3	3	3	45
Growing Churches	*	*	*	*	*	*	*	*	94
Static Churches	0	45	50	0	0	5	0	0	33
Declining Churches	*	*	*	*	*	*	*	*	52
Roman Catholic Churches	*	*	*	*	*	*	*	*	60

[1] This table is based on responses from 67% of all the churches in Orkney
[2] Where held, morning and evening services combined excluding twicers
[3] Percentages based on a small number of churches
* Too few churches to give a meaningful figure

SHETLAND ISLANDS

Total Adult Population:	17,340
Change of adult population in four years:	+11%
Total child population (under 15):	5,430
Change of child population in four years:	+13%
Total number of churches:	62
Percentage of churches responding:	82%
Total number of ministers:	58
Percentage of churches holding mid-week meetings:	60%
1984 adult Protestant church membership as percentage of total adult population:	24%
1984 Roman Catholic church membership as percentage of total adult population:	1%
1984 adult church attenders (Protestant and Roman Catholic) as percentage of total adult population:	14%
1984 adult church adherents as percentage of total adult population:	11%

Shetland

	Child Attenders			Adult Attenders			Membership			Average Sunday Congregation[1]
	1980	1984	Change	1980	1984	Change	1980	1984	Change	1984
			%			%			%	Adults
Church of Scotland	310	**390**	+26	930	**840**	−10	2,200	**2,060**	−6	60
Conservative Presbyterian	0	**0**	−	0	**0**	−	0	**0**	−	−
Scottish Episcopal	20	**20**	0	80	**90**	+13	260	**260**	0	43
Baptist	130	**160**	+23	230	**270**	+17	190	**190**	0	53
Independent	280	**290**	+4	570	**450**	−21	500	**410**	−18	45
Other Denominations	350	**320**	−9	670	**780**	+16	950	**1,010**	+6	26
TOTAL Protestant	1,090	**1,180**	+8	2,480	**2,430**	−2	4,100	**3,930**	−4	40
Roman Catholic	20	**20**	0	80	**70**	−12	180[3]	**180[3]**	0	70
TOTAL All Churches	1,110	**1,200**	+8	2,560	**2,500**	−2	4,280	**4,110**	−4	40

Age Group	Church Attenders[2]			Civil Population		
	Male	Female	Total	Male	Female	Total
	%	%	%	%	%	%
Under 15	12	18	30	12	12	24
15-19	3	3	6	4	4	8
20-29	3	5	8	8	7	15
30-44	5	9	14	11	10	21
45-64	6	11	17	9	9	18
65 or over	8	17	25	6	8	14
All ages	37	63	100	50	50	100

[1] Morning and evening congregations combined where both held excluding twicers
[2] This table is based on responses from 70% of all the Protestant churches in Shetland
[3] Total Catholic population including children

SHETLAND ISLANDS

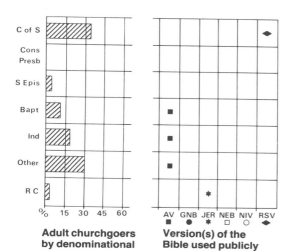

Morning only
Morning & evening
Evening only

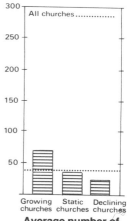

Adult churchgoers by denominational proportion

Version(s) of the Bible used publicly on Sunday

Proportion of Churches with morning and evening services

Average number of adults attending weekly services

Number of adult attenders[2]	Percentage of churches which between 1980 & 1984:			Version of the Bible most used:		1984 Adults attending twice on Sunday	1984 Churches whose Services were held:			Mid-week meetings 1984:	
	Grew	Remained Static	Declined	Sunday	Mid-week Meetings		Morning only	Morn. & Evening	Evening only	Churches with	Average attendance
	%	%	%			%	%	%	%	%	
Church of Scotland	23	62	15	RSV	Various	16	31	61	8	69	11
Conservative Presbyterian	–	–	–	–	–	–	–	–	–	–	–
Scottish Episcopal	*	*	*	*	*	*	0	100	0	*	*
Baptist[3]	33	67	0	AV	AV	47	0	33	67	50	35
Independent[3]	0	100	0	AV	AV	47	60	40	0	40	35
Other Denominations	29	57	14	AV	AV	30	29	35	36	62	15
All Protestant	24	62	14	AV	AV	39	31	42	27	61	16
Roman Catholic	*	*	*	JER	–	*	0	100	0	0	–
All Churches	24	62	14	AV	AV	37	30	44	26	60	16

Number of adult attenders[2]	1984 Sizes of Sunday Congregations[1]								Average Congregation per Church[2]
	Under 10	10-25	26-50	51-100	101-150	151-200	201-300	Over 300	
	%	%	%	%	%	%	%	%	
All Protestant Churches	20	33	20	23	2	0	2	0	40
Growing Churches	25	8	8	25	34	0	0	0	67
Static Churches	13	42	26	16	0	0	3	0	35
Declining Churches	*	*	*	*	*	*	*	*	90
Roman Catholic Churches	*	*	*	*	*	*	*	*	70

[1] This table is based on responses from 81% of all the churches in Shetland
[2] Where held, morning and evening services combined excluding twicers
[3] Percentages based on a small number of churches
* Too few churches to give a meaningful figure

STRATHCLYDE: DUMBARTON, CLYDEBANK AND CUMBERNAULD & KILSYTH

Total Adult Population:	144,650
Change of adult population in four years:	+4%
Total child population (under 15):	45,820
Change of child population in four years:	−6%
Total number of churches:	112
Percentage of churches responding:	78%
Total number of ministers:	115
Percentage of churches holding mid-week meetings:	70%
1984 adult Protestant church membership as percentage of total adult population:	19%
1984 Roman Catholic church membership as percentage of total adult population:	44%
1984 adult church attenders (Protestant and Roman Catholic) as percentage of total adult population:	24%
1984 adult church adherents as percentage of total adult population:	2%

Argyll · Tayside · Central · Fife · Strathclyde

1 Dumbarton
2 Clydebank
3 Cumbernauld & Kilsyth

	Child Attenders			Adult Attenders			Membership			Average Sunday Congregation[1]
	1980	1984	Change	1980	1984	Change	1980	1984	Change	1984
			%			%			%	Adults
Church of Scotland	2,780	2,920	+5	7,660	7,530	−2	23,640	22,560	−5	184
Conservative Presbyterian	70	70	0	190	190	0	280	270	−4	63
Scottish Episcopal	100	110	+10	430	450	+5	1,310	1,220	−7	89
Baptist	210	190	−10	460	460	0	500	460	−8	91
Independent	630	580	−8	1,230	1,060	−14	1,550	1,470	−5	66
Other Denominations	400	470	+18	1,090	1,070	−2	1,350	1,320	−2	67
TOTAL Protestant	4,190	4,340	+4	11,060	10,760	−3	28,630	27,300	−5	125
Roman Catholic	5,250	5,600	+7	21,900	23,350	+7	63,270[3]	63,900[3]	+1	898
TOTAL All Churches	9,440	9,940	+5	32,960	34,110	+3	91,900	91,200	−1	305

Age Group	Church Attenders[2]			Civil Population		
	Male	Female	Total	Male	Female	Total
	%	%	%	%	%	%
Under 15	12	15	27	12	12	24
15-19	3	4	7	5	4	9
20-29	3	5	8	7	8	15
30-44	5	10	15	10	10	20
45-64	7	15	22	10	11	21
65 or over	6	15	21	4	7	11
All ages	36	64	100	48	52	100

[1] Morning and evening congregations combined where both held excluding twicers
[2] This table is based on responses from 73% of all the Protestant churches in the Strathclyde districts given above
[3] Total Catholic population including children

STRATHCLYDE: DUMBARTON, CLYDEBANK AND CUMBERNAULD & KILSYTH

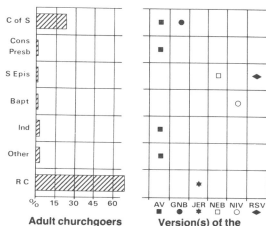

**Adult churchgoers
by denominational
proportion**

**Version(s) of the
Bible used publicly
on Sunday**

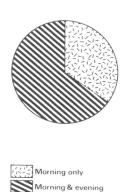

Morning only
Morning & evening
Evening only

**Proportion of
Churches with
morning and
evening services**

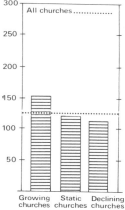

All churches...............

Growing Static Declining
churches churches churches

**Average number of
adults attending
weekly services**

	Percentage of churches which between 1980 & 1984:			Version of the Bible most used:		1984 Adults attending twice on Sunday	1984 Churches whose Services were held:			Mid-week meetings 1984:	
	Grew	Remained Static	Declined	Sunday	Mid-week Meetings		Morning only	Morn. & Evening	Evening only	Churches with	Average attendance
	%	%	%			%	%	%	%	%	
Church of Scotland	20	47	33	AV/GNB	GNB	5	67	33	0	67	19
Conservative Presbyterian[3]	33	67	0	AV	AV/NIV	40	0	100	0	67	22
Scottish Episcopal[3]	40	60	0	NEB/RSV	GNB/RSV	14	60	40	0	80	21
Baptist[3]	0	100	0	NIV	NIV	44	0	100	0	100	23
Independent	8	77	15	AV	AV	41	23	77	0	85	21
Other Denominations	47	47	6	AV	AV	32	20	80	0	80	12
All Protestant	25	57	18	AV	AV	19	44	56	0	75	18
Roman Catholic	47	35	18	JER	JER	3	0	100	0	50	63
All Churches	29	52	19	AV	GNB	7	35	65	0	70	25

	1984 Sizes of Sunday Congregations[1]								Average Congregation per Church[2]
Number of adult attenders[2]	Under 10	10-25	26-50	51-100	101-150	151-200	201-300	Over 300	
	%	%	%	%	%	%	%	%	
All Protestant Churches	0	7	22	28	11	17	9	6	125
Growing Churches	0	0	24	28	6	12	18	12	151
Static Churches	0	13	23	15	10	26	8	5	119
Declining Churches	0	0	15	15	55	15	0	0	112
Roman Catholic Churches	0	0	0	6	0	0	0	94	898

[1] This table is based on responses from 77% of all the churches in Dumbarton, Clydebank and Cumbernauld & Kilsyth
[2] Morning and evening services combined, where both held, excluding twicers
[3] Percentage unreliable because based on a particularly small number of churches

STRATHCLYDE: EAST KILBRIDE, HAMILTON AND LANARK

Total Adult Population:	189,710
Change of adult population in four years:	+6%
Total child population (under 15):	57,430
Change of child population in four years:	−6%
Total number of churches:	161
Percentage of churches responding:	68%
Total number of ministers:	127
Percentage of churches holding mid-week meetings:	65%
1984 adult Protestant church membership as percentage of total adult population:	24%
1984 Roman Catholic church membership as percentage of total adult population:	26%
1984 adult church attenders (Protestant and Roman Catholic) as percentage of total adult population:	19%
1984 adult church adherents as percentage of total adult population:	1%

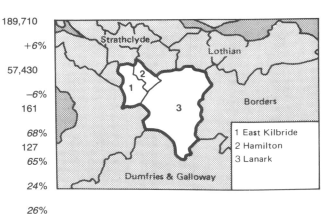

1 East Kilbride
2 Hamilton
3 Lanark

	Child Attenders			Adult Attenders			Membership			Average Sunday Congregation[1]
	1980	1984	Change	1980	1984	Change	1980	1984	Change	1984
			%			%			%	Adults
Church of Scotland	4,180	**4,790**	+15	11,260	**11,840**	+5	39,670	**38,250**	−4	174
Conservative Presbyterian	10	**10**	0	30	**30**	0	60	**60**	0	15
Presbyterian Scottish Episcopal	50	**70**	+40	380	**370**	−3	950	**850**	−11	75
Baptist	770	**690**	−10	1,580	**1,430**	−9	1,430	**1,450**	+1	159
Independent	1,640	**1,350**	−18	2,500	**2,100**	−16	3,480	**3,270**	−6	57
Other Denominations	460	**440**	−4	650	**750**	+15	900	**930**	+3	50
TOTAL Protestant	7,110	**7,350**	+3	16,400	**16,520**	+1	46,490	**44,810**	−4	122
Roman Catholic	4,570	**4,590**	0	19,020	**19,140**	+1	50,940[3]	**49,250[3]**	−3	766
TOTAL All Churches	11,680	**11,940**	+2	35,420	**35,660**	+1	97,430	**94,060**	−3	221

	Church Attenders[2]			Civil Population		
Age Group	Male	Female	Total	Male	Female	Total
	%	%	%	%	%	%
Under 15	12	17	29	12	11	23
15-19	2	4	6	5	4	9
20-29	3	6	9	7	8	15
30-44	6	10	16	10	10	20
45-64	8	15	23	11	11	22
65 or over	6	11	17	4	7	11
All ages	37	63	100	49	51	100

[1] Morning and evening congregations combined where both held excluding twicers
[2] This table is based on responses from 63% of all the Protestant churches in East Kilbride, Hamilton and Lanark
[3] Total Catholic population including children

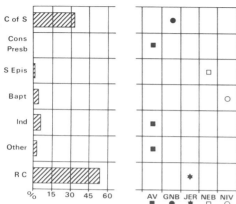

Adult churchgoers by denominational proportion

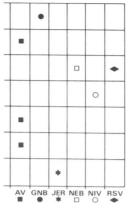

Version(s) of the Bible used publicly on Sunday

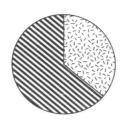

Morning only

Morning & evening

Evening only

Proportion of Churches with morning and evening services

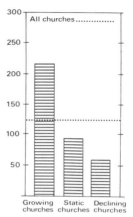

Average number of adults attending weekly services

Number of adult attenders[2]	Percentage of churches which between 1980 & 1984:			Version of the Bible most used:		1984 Adults attending twice on Sunday	1984 Churches whose Services were held:			Mid-week meetings 1984:	
	Grew	Remained Static	Declined	Sunday	Mid-week Meetings		Morning only	Morn. & Evening	Evening only	Churches with	Average attendance
	%	%	%			%	%	%	%	%	
Church of Scotland	45	30	25	GNB	GNB	8	57	43	0	56	18
Conservative Presbyterian	*	*	*	AV	AV	71	50	50	0	50	13
Scottish Episcopal	*	*	*	NEB/RSV	GNB/RSV	*	100	0	0	100	8
Baptist[3]	25	75	0	NIV	NIV	43	0	100	0	100	45
Independent	7	79	14	AV	AV	53	21	79	0	79	32
Other Denominations	27	73	0	AV	AV/NIV	45	36	64	0	73	13
All Protestant	28	56	16	AV	AV	24	39	61	0	69	25
Roman Catholic	14	57	29	JER	JER	1	14	83	0	43	27
All Churches	27	56	17	AV	AV	11	36	64	0	65	25

Number of adult attenders[2]	1984 Sizes of Sunday Congregations[1]								Average Congregation per Church[2]
	Under 10	10-25	26-50	51-100	101-150	151-200	201-300	Over 300	
	%	%	%	%	%	%	%	%	
All Protestant Churches	3	6	24	22	15	11	12	7	122
Growing Churches	0	0	4	22	4	15	37	18	214
Static Churches	4	9	30	19	21	11	2	4	93
Declining Churches	7	7	40	33	13	0	0	0	57
Roman Catholic Churches	0	14	0	7	7	0	7	65	766

[1] This table is based on responses from 68% of all the churches in East Kilbride, Hamilton and Lanark
[2] Morning and evening services combined where both held excluding twicers
[3] Percentages unreliable because based on a particularly small number of churches
* Too few churches to give a meaningful figure

STRATHCLYDE: EASTWOOD, BEARSDEN & MILNGAVIE, AND STRATHKELVIN

Total Adult Population:	138,030
Change of adult population in four years:	+6%
Total child population (under 15):	41,360
Change of child population in four years:	−3%
Total number of churches:	75
Percentage of churches responding:	72%
Total number of ministers:	71
Percentage of churches holding mid-week meetings:	81%
1984 adult Protestant church membership as percentage of total adult population:	22%
1984 Roman Catholic church membership as percentage of total adult population:	30%
1984 adult church attenders (Protestant and Roman Catholic) as percentage of total adult population:	20%
1984 adult church adherents as percentage of total adult population:	1%

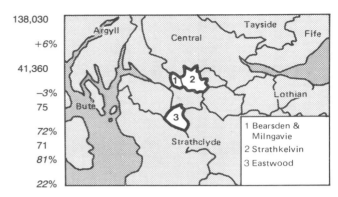

1 Bearsden & Milngavie
2 Strathkelvin
3 Eastwood

	Child Attenders			Adult Attenders			Membership			Average Sunday Congregation[1]
	1980	1984	Change	1980	1984	Change	1980	1984	Change	1984
			%			%			%	Adults
Church of Scotland	4,960	5,070	+2	9,440	9,620	+2	27,780	27,880	0	291
Conservative Presbyterian	10	10	0	40	40	0	40	40	0	39
Scottish Episcopal	130	120	−8	420	370	−12	1,090	1,000	−8	74
Baptist	320	280	−13	480	540	+13	440	540	+23	135
Independent	530	420	−21	930	810	−12	710	730	+3	101
Other Denominations	190	170	−11	410	310	−24	580	480	−17	62
TOTAL Protestant	6,140	6,070	−1	11,720	11,690	0	30,640	30,670	0	209
Roman Catholic	3,320	3,830	+15	13,840	15,960	+15	35,050[3]	40,610[3]	+16	840
TOTAL All Churches	9,460	9,900	+5	25,560	27,650	+8	65,720	71,280	+8	369

Age Group	Church Attenders[2]			Civil Population		
	Male	Female	Total	Male	Female	Total
	%	%	%	%	%	%
Under 15	15	17	32	12	11	23
15-19	3	5	8	5	4	9
20-29	3	6	9	6	7	13
30-44	7	11	18	11	11	22
45-64	9	12	21	10	12	22
65 or over	4	8	12	4	7	11
All ages	41	59	100	48	52	100

[1] Morning and evening congregations combined where both held excluding twicers
[2] This table is based on responses from 64% of all the Protestant churches in the Strathclyde districts given above
[3] Total Catholic population including children

STRATHCLYDE: EASTWOOD, BEARSDEN & MILNGAVIE, AND STRATHKELVIN

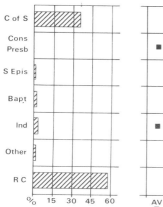

Adult churchgoers by denominational proportion

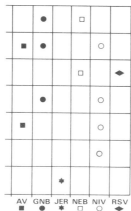

Version(s) of the Bible used publicly on Sunday

Morning only
Morning & evening
Evening only

Proportion of Churches with morning and evening services

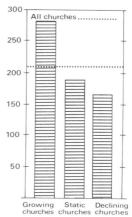

Average number of adults attending weekly services

	Percentage of churches which between 1980 & 1984:			Version of the Bible most used:		1984 Adults attending twice on Sunday	1984 Churches whose Services were held:			Mid-week meetings 1984:	
	Grew	Remained Static	Declined	Sunday	Mid-week Meetings		Morning only	Morn. & Evening	Evening only	Churches with	Average attendance
	%	%	%			%	%	%	%	%	
Church of Scotland	28	55	17	GNB/NEB	GNB	10	55	45	0	86	20
Conservative Presbyterian	*	*	*	Various	NIV	35	0	100	0	100	22
Scottish Episcopal[3]	20	60	20	NEB/RSV	GNB/NEB	11	0	100	0	100	10
Baptist[3]	67	33	0	GNB/NIV	GNB/NIV	50	0	100	0	100	48
Independent	*	*	*	AV	AV	46	0	100	0	100	38
Other Denominations[3]	0	100	0	NIV	NIV/AV	32	0	100	0	100	10
All Protestant	25	61	14	GNB/NEB	GNB	15	36	64	0	91	21
Roman Catholic	40	50	10	JER	JER/GNB	3	10	90	0	25	10
All Churches	28	59	13	GNB	GNB	9	31	69	0	81	21

Number of adult attenders[2]	1984 Sizes of Sunday Congregations[1]								Average Congregation per Church[2]
	Under 10	10-25	26-50	51-100	101-150	151-200	201-300	Over 300	
	%	%	%	%	%	%	%	%	
All Protestant Churches	0	4	7	18	16	11	14	30	209
Growing Churches	0	0	0	27	0	0	18	55	285
Static Churches	0	8	11	15	22	7	11	26	188
Declining Churches	*	*	*	*	*	*	*	*	162
Roman Catholic Churches	0	0	0	0	0	10	20	70	840

[1] This table is based on responses from 72% of all the churches in Strathclyde districts named above
[2] Morning and evening services combined where both held excluding twicers
[3] Percentages unreliable because based on a particularly small number of churches
* Too few churches to give a meaningful figure

STRATHCLYDE: GLASGOW

Total Adult Population:	606,100
Change of adult population in four years:	−7%
Total child population (under 15):	149,330
Change of child population in four years:	−19%
Total number of churches:	390
Percentage of churches responding:	76%
Total number of ministers:	424
Percentage of churches holding mid-week meetings:	66%
1984 adult Protestant church membership as percentage of total adult population:	16%
1984 Roman Catholic church membership as percentage of total adult population:	38%
1984 adult church attenders (Protestant and Roman Catholic) as percentage of total adult population:	19%
1984 adult church adherents as percentage of total adult population:	1%

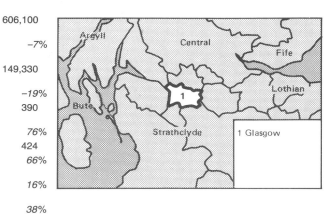

1 Glasgow

	Child Attenders			Adult Attenders			Membership			Average Sunday Congregation[1]
	1980	1984	Change	1980	1984	Change	1980	1984	Change	1984
			%			%			%	Adults
Church of Scotland	12,430	9,870	−21	35,550	31,200	−12	89,760	79,920	−11	212
Conservative Presbyterian	260	240	−8	1,210	1,070	−12	1,700	1,540	−9	97
Scottish Episcopal	240	300	+25	1,350	1,290	−4	3,290	2,780	−16	72
Baptist	900	760	−16	2,850	2,570	−10	2,670	2,630	−1	112
Independent	1,310	1,140	−13	3,020	2,800	−7	4,860	4,510	−7	74
Other Denominations	1,440	1,630	+13	4,830	4,390	−9	6,060	5,500	−4	70
TOTAL Protestant	16,580	13,940	−16	48,840	43,320	−11	108,340	97,180	−10	144
Roman Catholic	18,270	17,380	−5	76,000	72,390	−5	233,690[3]	231,690[3]	−1	804
TOTAL All Churches	34,850	31,320	−10	124,840	115,710	−7	342,030	328,870	−4	297

Age Group	Church Attenders[2]			Civil Population		
	Male	Female	Total	Male	Female	Total
	%	%	%	%	%	%
Under 15	10	13	23	10	10	20
15-19	2	3	5	5	4	9
20-29	4	5	9	5	8	16
30-44	5	9	14	8	8	16
45-64	8	17	25	11	12	23
65 or over	7	17	24	6	10	19
All ages	36	64	100	48	52	100

[1] Morning and evening congregations combined where both held excluding twicers
[2] This table is based on responses from 67% of all the Protestant churches in Glasgow
[3] Total Catholic population including children

STRATHCLYDE: GLASGOW

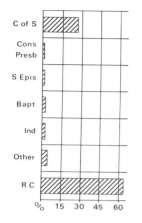

Adult churchgoers by denominational proportion

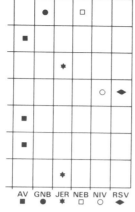

Version(s) of the Bible used publicly on Sunday

Proportion of Churches with morning and evening services

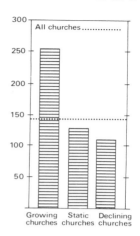

Average number of adults attending weekly services

	Percentage of churches which between 1980 & 1984:			Version of the Bible most used:		1984 Adults attending twice on Sunday	1984 Churches whose Services were held:			Mid-week meetings 1984:	
	Grew	Remained Static	Declined	Sunday	Mid-week Meetings		Morning only	Morn. & Evening	Evening only	Churches with	Average attendance
	%	%	%		%	%	%	%	%	%	
Church of Scotland	25	36	39	NEB/GNB	GNB	10	44	56	0	69	19
Conservative Presbyterian[3]	22	45	33	AV	AV	59	11	89	0	100	27
Scottish Episcopal[3]	14	72	14	JER	GNB	11	14	86	0	71	9
Baptist	38	38	24	RSV/NIV	RSV	35	0	100	0	100	33
Independent	26	67	7	AV	AV	33	22	78	0	70	30
Other Denominations	25	62	13	AV	AV/GNB	37	13	72	15	60	18
All Protestant	26	47	27	AV	GNB	22	32	65	3	72	22
Roman Catholic	18	46	36	JER	JER	3	2	98	0	43	81
All Churches	24	47	29	AV	GNB	9	25	72	3	66	30

Number of adult attenders[2]	1984 Sizes of Sunday Congregations[1]								Average Congregation per Church[2]
	Under 10	10-25	26-50	51-100	101-150	151-200	201-300	Over 300	
	%	%	%	%	%	%	%	%	
All Protestant Churches	1	5	13	28	17	9	12	15	144
Growing Churches	2	2	2	15	17	8	8	46	252
Static Churches	1	8	22	26	9	8	20	6	128
Declining Churches	0	3	8	41	32	11	3	2	109
Roman Catholic Churches	0	0	0	0	0	2	5	93	804

[1] This table is based on responses from 75% of all the churches in Glasgow
[2] Morning and evening services combined where both held excluding twicers
[3] Percentages unreliable because based on a particularly small number of churches

STRATHCLYDE: KYLE & CARRICK, CUMNOCH & DOUN VALLEY, KILMARNOCK & LOUDOUN, AND CUNNINGHAME

Total Adult Population:	292,030
Change of adult population in four years:	+3%
Total child population (under 15):	83,030
Change of child population in four years:	−5%
Total number of churches:	272
Percentage of churches responding:	73%
Total number of ministers:	248
Percentage of churches holding mid-week meetings:	57%
1984 adult Protestant church membership as percentage of total adult population:	30%
1984 Roman Catholic church membership as percentage of total adult population:	16%
1984 adult church attenders (Protestant and Roman Catholic) as percentage of total adult population:	16%
1984 adult church adherents as percentage of total adult population:	1%

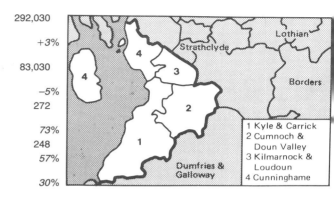

1 Kyle & Carrick
2 Cumnoch & Doun Valley
3 Kilmarnock & Loudoun
4 Cunninghame

	Child Attenders			Adult Attenders			Membership			Average Sunday Congregation[1]
	1980	1984	Change	1980	1984	Change	1980	1984	Change	1984
			%			%			%	Adults
Church of Scotland	8,200	8,870	+8	25,100	25,040	0	81,990	77,850	−5	204
Conservative Presbyterian	60	60	0	150	130	−13	190	170	−11	17
Scottish Episcopal	190	250	+32	690	600	−13	2,390	2,230	−7	50
Baptist	390	440	+13	1,310	1,480	+13	1,150	1,200	+4	134
Independent	1,860	1,690	−9	3,470	3,300	−5	4,110	4,170	+1	67
Other Denominations	680	790	+16	1,800	1,720	−4	2,550	2,440	−4	59
TOTAL Protestant	11,380	12,100	+6	32,520	32,270	−1	92,380	88,060	−5	139
Roman Catholic	3,980	3,780	−5	16,580	15,750	−5	47,570[3]	44,890[3]	−6	394
TOTAL All Churches	15,360	15,880	+3	49,100	48,020	−2	139,950	132,950	−5	177

	Church Attenders[2]			Civil Population		
Age Group	Male	Female	Total	Male	Female	Total
	%	%	%	%	%	%
Under 15	12	14	26	11	11	22
15-19	2	4	6	5	4	9
20-29	3	6	9	7	7	14
30-44	5	10	15	9	10	19
45-64	8	14	22	10	12	22
65 or over	8	14	22	6	8	14
All ages	38	62	100	48	52	100

[1] Morning and evening congregations combined where both held excluding twicers
[2] This table is based on responses from 65% of all the Protestant churches in the Strathclyde districts given above
[3] Total Catholic population including children

STRATHCLYDE: KYLE & CARRICK, CUMNOCH & DOUN VALLEY, KILMARNOCK & LOUDOUN, AND CUNNINGHAME

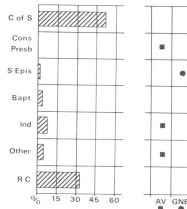

Adult churchgoers by denominational proportion

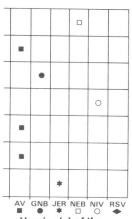

Version(s) of the Bible used publicly on Sunday

Proportion of Churches with morning and evening services

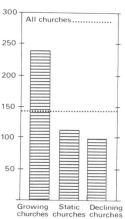

Average number of adults attending weekly services

	Percentage of churches which between 1980 & 1984:			Version of the Bible most used:		1984 Adults attending twice on Sunday	1984 Churches whose Services were held:			Mid-week meetings 1984:	
	Grew	Remained Static	Declined	Sunday	Mid-week Meetings		Morning only	Morn. & Evening	Evening only	Churches with	Average attendance
	%	%	%			%	%	%	%	%	
Church of Scotland	32	43	25	NEB	NEB	9	58	42	0	49	18
Conservative Presbyterian[1]	0	100	0	AV	AV	31	50	33	17	42	12
Presbyterian											
Scottish Episcopal[1]	0	83	17	GNB	GNB/JER	16	17	83	0	50	11
Baptist[1]	50	33	17	NIV	NIV	31	0	100	0	100	32
Independent	17	79	4	AV	AV	43	21	79	0	84	27
Other Denominations	32	64	4	AV	AV	40	43	53	4	54	19
All Protestant	28	55	17	AV	AV	21	46	53	1	57	21
Roman Catholic	11	61	28	JER	JER	7	21	79	0	57	22
All Churches	26	56	18	AV	AV	16	43	56	1	57	21

	1984 Sizes of Sunday Congregations[2]								Average Congregation per Church[3]
Number of adult attenders[3]	Under 10	10-25	26-50	51-100	101-150	151-200	201-300	Over 300	
	%	%	%	%	%	%	%	%	
All Protestant Churches	4	9	16	21	9	13	15	13	139
Growing Churches	4	4	2	11	9	13	21	36	240
Static Churches	5	12	25	20	8	10	16	4	110
Declining Churches	0	7	10	45	14	24	0	0	98
Roman Catholic Churches	0	0	4	18	4	7	7	60	394

[1] Percentages unreliable because based on a particularly small number of churches
[2] This table is based on responses from 72% of all the churches in the Strathclyde districts given above
[3] Morning and evening services combined where both held excluding twicers

STRATHCLYDE: MOTHERWELL AND MONKLANDS

Total adult Population:	197,640
Change of adult population in four years:	+1%
Total child population (under 15):	61,700
Change of child population in four years:	-9%
Total number of churches:	178
Percentage of churches responding:	80%
Total number of ministers:	181
Percentage of churches holding mid-week meetings:	64%
1984 adult Protestant church membership as percentage of total adult population:	21%
1984 Roman Catholic church membership as percentage of total adult population:	47%
1984 adult church attenders (Protestant and Roman Catholic) as percentage of total adult population:	27%
1984 adult church adherents as percentage of total adult population:	1%

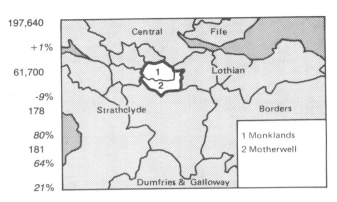

1 Monklands
2 Motherwell

	Child Attenders			Adult Attenders			Membership			Average Sunday Congregation[1]
	1980	1984	Change	1980	1984	Change	1980	1984	Change	1984
			%			%			%	Adults
Church of Scotland	4,240	4,050	-4	11,430	11,320	-1	35,960	33,750	-6	195
Conservative Presbyterian	20	30	†	100	90	-10	170	150	-12	28
Presbyterian Scottish Episcopal	30	40	+33	240	170	-29	630	450	-29	34
Baptist	530	500	-6	1,620	1,470	-9	1,380	1,430	+4	210
Independent	1,420	1,250	-12	2,990	2,820	-6	3,610	3,370	-7	71
Other Denominations	740	610	-18	1,770	1,600	-10	1,840	1,740	-5	67
TOTAL Protestant	6,980	6,480	-7	18,150	17,470	-4	43,590	40,890	-6	127
Roman Catholic	9,290	8,850	-5	38,690	36,880	-5	89,620[3]	93,160[3]	+4	900
TOTAL All Churches	16,270	15,330	-6	56,840	54,650	-4	133,210	134,050	+1	305

	Church Attenders[2]			Civil Population		
Age Group	Male	Female	Total	Male	Female	Total
	%	%	%	%	%	%
Under 15	11	15	26	12	12	24
15-19	2	4	6	5	5	10
20-29	4	6	10	8	7	15
30-44	6	10	16	9	9	18
45-64	8	14	22	10	12	22
65 or over	7	13	20	4	7	11
All ages	7	13	20	4	7	11

[1] Morning and evening congregations combined where both held excluding twicers
[2] This table is based on responses from 73% of all the Protestant churches in Motherwell and Monklands
[3] Total Catholic population including children
† Numbers too small to give a meaningful percentage

STRATHCLYDE: MOTHERWELL AND MONKLANDS

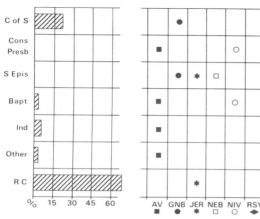

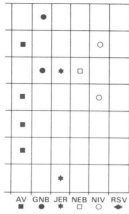

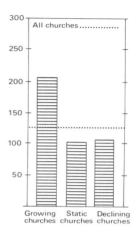

Adult churchgoers by denominational proportion

Version(s) of the Bible used publicly on Sunday

Proportion of Churches with morning and evening services

Average number of adults attending weekly services

	Percentage of churches which between 1980 & 1984:			Version of the Bible most used:		1984 Adults attending twice on Sunday	1984 Churches whose Services were held:			Mid-week meetings 1984:	
	Grew	Remained Static	Declined	Sunday	Mid-week Meetings		Morning only	Morn. & Evening	Evening only	Churches with	Average attendance
	%	%	%			%	%	%	%	%	
Church of Scotland	34	45	21	GNB	GNB	8	36	64	0	64	21
Conservative Presbyterian[3]	0	100	0	AV/NIV	AV/NIV	34	0	100	0	100	9
Scottish Episcopal[3]	0	75	25	Various	NEB	*	100	0	0	25	6
Baptist	*	*	*	AV/NIV	AV/NIV	41	0	100	0	100	58
Independent	19	65	16	AV	AV	37	23	74	3	77	29
Other Denominations	18	77	5	AV	AV	35	36	64	0	61	18
TOTAL Protestant	26	59	15	AV	AV	22	33	66	1	67	23
Roman Catholic	17	59	24	JER	JER	1	0	100	0	52	29
TOTAL All Churches	24	59	17	AV	AV	7	26	73	1	64	24

Number of adult attenders[2]	1984 Sizes of Sunday Congregations[1]								Average Congregation per Church[2]
	Under 10	10-25	26-50	51-100	101-150	151-200	201-300	Over 300	
	%	%	%	%	%	%	%	%	
All Protestant Churches	6	8	16	16	17	17	15	5	127
Growing Churches	0	4	0	14	18	14	36	14	204
Static Churches	8	13	28	11	8	20	9	3	100
Declining Churches	6	0	0	35	53	6	0	0	103
Roman Catholic Churches	0	0	0	3	0	3	0	94	900

[1] This table is based on responses from 78% of all the churches in Motherwell and Monklands
[2] Morning and evening services combined where both held excluding twicers
[3] Percentage unreliable because based on a particularly small number of churches
* Too few churches to give a meaningful figure

STRATHCLYDE: RENFREW AND INVERCLYDE

Total Adult Population:	237,460
Change of adult population in four years:	+2%
Total child population (under 15):	67,430
Change of child population in four years:	−10%
Total number of churches:	172
Percentage of churches responding:	73%
Total number of ministers:	162
Percentage of churches holding mid-week meetings:	66%
1984 adult Protestant church membership as percentage of total adult population:	25%
1984 Roman Catholic church membership as percentage of total adult population:	38%
1984 adult church attenders (Protestant and Roman Catholic) as percentage of total adult population:	22%
1984 adult church adherents as percentage of total adult population:	1%

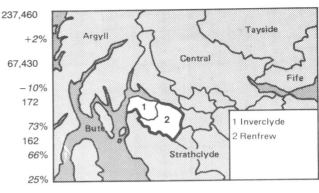

1 Inverclyde
2 Renfrew

	Child Attenders			Adult Attenders			Membership			Average Sunday Congregation[1]
	1980	1984	Change	1980	1984	Change	1980	1984	Change	1984
			%			%			%	Adults
Church of Scotland	6,420	**5,860**	−9	19,090	**17,020**	−11	54,290	**50,230**	−7	240
Conservative Presbyterian	30	**30**	0	160	**130**	−19	220	**180**	−18	44
Scottish Episcopal	130	**190**	+46	530	**570**	+8	2,170	**1,940**	−11	72
Baptist	510	**450**	−12	1,120	**1,030**	−8	1,050	**930**	−11	86
Independent	870	**850**	−2	1,760	**1,570**	−11	2,800	**2,380**	−15	65
Other Denominations	910	**970**	+7	1,970	**2,010**	+2	2,490	**2,550**	+2	101
TOTAL Protestant	8,870	**8,350**	−6	24,630	**22,330**	−9	63,020	**58,210**	−8	159
Roman Catholic	7,640	**7,420**	−3	31,850	**30,940**	−3	88,950[3]	**90,310**[3]	+2	910
TOTAL All Churches	16,510	**15,770**	−4	56,480	**53,270**	−6	151,970	**148,520**	−2	310

Age Group	Church Attenders[2]			Civil Population		
	Male	Female	Total	Male	Female	Total
	%	%	%	%	%	%
Under 15	11	13	24	11	11	22
15-19	2	4	6	5	5	10
20-29	3	6	9	8	7	15
30-44	5	11	16	9	10	19
45-64	9	16	25	11	11	22
65 or over	7	13	20	4	8	12
All ages	37	63	100	48	52	100

[1] Morning and evening congregations combined where both held excluding twicers
[2] This table is based on responses from 67% of all the Protestant churches in Renfrew and Inverclyde
[3] Total Catholic population including children

STRATHCLYDE: RENFREW AND INVERCLYDE

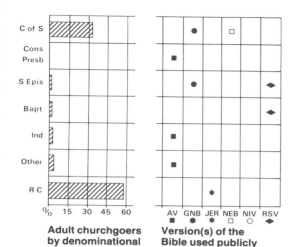

Adult churchgoers by denominational proportion

Version(s) of the Bible used publicly on Sunday

Morning only

Morning & evening

Evening only

Proportion of Churches with morning and evening services

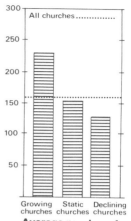

Average number of adults attending weekly services

	Percentage of churches which between 1980 & 1984:			Version of the Bible most used:		1984 Adults attending twice on Sunday	1984 Churches whose Services were held:			Mid-week meetings 1984:	
	Grew	Remained Static	Declined	Sunday	Mid-week Meetings		Morning only	Morn. & Evening	Evening only	Churches with	Average attendance
	%	%	%			%	%	%	%	%	
Church of Scotland	24	36	40	GNB/NEB	GNB	8	43	57	0	55	17
Conservative Presbyterian[3]	33	34	33	AV	AV	57	0	100	0	67	20
Scottish Episcopal[3]	40	60	0	GNB/RSV	GNB	16	20	80	0	60	11
Baptist[3]	33	67	0	RSV	RSV	41	0	100	0	100	19
Independent	9	73	18	AV	AV	27	18	82	0	91	25
Other Denominations	19	75	6	AV	AV	45	13	87	0	81	16
All Protestant	24	50	26	GNB	GNB	18	29	71	0	68	18
Roman Catholic	9	70	21	JER	JER	6	9	91	0	60	26
All Churches	21	54	25	GNB	GNB	11	26	74	0	66	19

Number of adult attenders[2]	1984 Sizes of Sunday Congregations[1]								Average Congregation per Church[2]
	Under 10	10-25	26-50	51-100	101-150	151-200	201-300	Over 300	
	%	%	%	%	%	%	%	%	
All Protestant Churches	0	4	15	19	18	14	18	12	159
Growing Churches	0	0	4	17	29	4	8	38	229
Static Churches	0	4	23	18	12	8	27	8	151
Declining Churches	0	7	7	23	23	33	7	0	125
Roman Catholic Churches	0	0	0	0	4	0	9	87	910

This table is based on responses from 73% of all the churches in Renfrew and Inverclyde
Morning and evening services combined where both held excluding twicers
Percentages unreliable because based on a particularly small number of churches

TAYSIDE: DUNDEE

Total Adult Population:	142,320
Change of adult population in four years:	−1%
Total child population (under 15):	35,230
Change of child population in four years:	−13%
Total number of churches:	109
Percentage of churches responding:	82%
Total number of ministers:	114
Percentage of churches holding mid-week meetings:	59%
1984 adult Protestant church membership as percentage of total adult population:	27%
1984 Roman Catholic church membership as percentage of total adult population:	19%
1984 adult church attenders (Protestant and Roman Catholic) as percentage of total adult population:	12%
1984 adult church adherents as percentage of total adult population:	2%

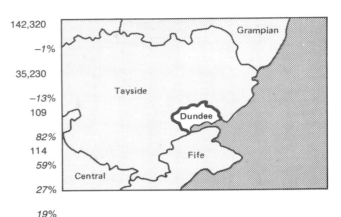

	Child Attenders			Adult Attenders			Membership			Average Sunday Congregation[1]
	1980	1984	Change	1980	1984	Change	1980	1984	Change	1984
			%			%			%	Adults
Church of Scotland	2,600	**2,570**	−1	6,670	**7,140**	+7	35,190	**34,300**	−3	143
Conservative Presbyterian	10	**0**	†	30	**40**	†	30	**50**	†	20
Scottish Episcopal	200	**220**	+10	780	**820**	+5	2,270	**2,300**	+1	69
Baptist	210	**190**	−10	720	**610**	−15	620	**580**	−6	102
Independent	140	**150**	+7	750	**610**	−19	870	**700**	−20	68
Other Denominations	200	**170**	−15	480	**550**	+15	800	**840**	+5	46
TOTAL Denominations	3,360	**3,300**	−2	9,430	**9,770**	+4	39,780	**38,770**	−3	107
Roman Catholic	2,030	**1,920**	−5	8,470	**7,990**	−6	28,010[3]	**26,890**[3]	−4	444
TOTAL All Churches	5,390	**5,220**	−3	17,900	**17,760**	−1	67,790	**65,660**	−3	163

	Church Attenders[2]			Civil Population		
Age Group	Male	Female	Total	Male	Female	Total
	%	%	%	%	%	%
Under 15	9	13	22	10	10	20
15-19	3	3	6	5	4	9
20-29	3	6	9	7	8	15
30-44	5	10	15	9	9	18
45-64	9	15	24	11	12	23
65 or over	7	17	24	5	10	15
All ages	36	64	100	47	53	100

[1] Morning and evening congregations combined where both held excluding twicers
[2] This table is based on responses from 73% of all the Protestant churches in Dundee
[3] Total Catholic population including children
† Numbers too small to give a meaningful percentage

TAYSIDE: DUNDEE

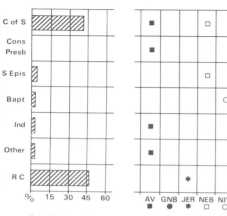

Adult churchgoers by denominational proportion

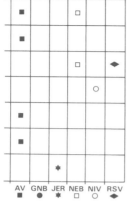

Version(s) of the Bible used publicly on Sunday

Morning only
Morning & evening
Evening only

Proportion of Churches with morning and evening services

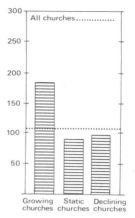

Average number of adults attending weekly services

	Percentage of churches which between 1980 & 1984:			Version of the Bible most used:		1984 Adults attending twice on Sunday	1984 Churches whose Services were held:			Mid-week meetings 1984:	
	Grew	Remained Static	Declined	Sunday	Mid-week Meetings		Morning only	Morn. & Evening	Evening only	Churches with	Average attendance
	%	%	%			%	%	%	%	%	
Church of Scotland	26	53	21	AV/NEB	GNB	13	67	33	0	40	18
Conservative Presbyterian	*	*	*	AV	AV	72	0	100	0	50	8
Scottish Episcopal[3]	29	71	0	NEB/RSV	GNB	11	57	43	0	86	10
Baptist[3]	17	83	0	NIV	NIV	46	0	100	0	100	19
Independent[3]	13	74	13	AV	AV/NIV	44	50	50	0	88	31
Other Denominations[3]	22	78	0	AV	AV	32	22	56	22	67	16
All Protestant	23	64	13	AV	AV/GNB	30	52	45	3	57	19
Roman Catholic	7	71	22	JER	JER	2	14	86	0	69	18
All Churches	20	65	15	AV	GNB	16	46	52	2	59	19

	1984 Sizes of Sunday Congregations[1]								Average Congregation per Church[2]
No. of adult attenders[2]	Under 10	10-25	26-50	51-100	101-150	151-200	201-300	Over 300	
	%	%	%	%	%	%	%	%	
All Protestant Churches	1	8	19	20	33	5	11	3	107
Growing Churches	6	0	0	12	28	18	24	12	184
Static Churches	0	13	23	21	35	2	6	0	88
Declining Churches	0	0	30	30	30	0	10	3	96
Roman Catholic Churches	0	0	0	0	0	0	17	83	444

¹ This table is based on responses from 82% of all the churchhes in Dundee
² Morning and evening services combined where both held excluding twicers
³ Percentages unreliable because based on a particularly small number of churches
* Too few churches to give a meaningful figure

TAYSIDE: OTHER

Total Adult Population:	162,930
Change of adult population in four years:	+2%
Total child population (under 15):	42,240
Change of child population in four years:	-4%
Total number of churches:	233
Percentage of churches responding:	78%
Total number of ministers:	224
Percentage of churches holding mid-week meetings:	45%
1984 adult Protestant church membership as percentage of total adult population:	45%
1984 Roman Catholic church membership as percentage of total adult population:	5%
1984 adult church attenders (Protestant and Roman Catholic) as percentage of total adult population:	12%
1984 adult church adherents as percentage of total adult population:	2%

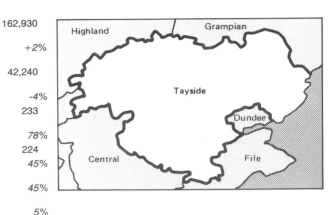

	Child Attenders			Adult Attenders			Membership			Average Sunday Congregation[1]
	1980	1984	Change	1980	1984	Change	1980	1984	Change	1984
			%			%			%	Adults
Church of Scotland	4,800	4,230	− 12	13,260	13,340	+ 1	67,960	65,800	− 3	102
Conservative Presbyterian	50	30	†	110	100	− 9	130	130	0	25
Scottish Episcopal	180	240	+33	1,040	980	− 6	2,810	3,010	+7	42
Baptist	250	310	+24	570	540	− 5	470	540	+15	60
Independent	200	250	+25	460	550	+20	1,190	1,120	− 6	28
Other Denominations	330	340	+3	1,150	1,040	− 10	1,990	1,860	− 7	39
TOTAL Protestant	5,810	5,400	− 7	16,590	16,550	0	74,550	72,460	− 3	77
Roman Catholic	830	750	− 10	3,480	3,100	− 11	7,760[3]	8,460[3]	+9	163
TOTAL All Churches	6,640	6,150	− 7	20,070	19,650	− 2	82,310	80,920	− 2	84

	Church Attenders[2]			Civil Population		
Age Group	Male	Female	Total	Male	Female	Total
	%	%	%	%	%	%
Under 15	10	12	22	10	10	20
15-19	2	3	5	4	4	8
20-29	3	6	9	7	6	13
30-44	6	10	16	9	10	19
45-64	9	15	24	11	12	23
65 or over	8	16	24	7	10	17
All ages	38	62	100	48	52	100

[1] Morning and evening congregations combined where both held excluding twicers
[2] This table is based on responses from 71% of all the Protestant churches in Tayside other than Dundee
[3] Total Catholic population including children
† Numbers too small to give a meaningful percentage

TAYSIDE: OTHER

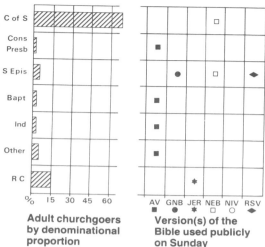

Adult churchgoers by denominational proportion

Version(s) of the Bible used publicly on Sunday

AV GNB JER NEB NIV RSV
■ ● ✳ □ ○ ◆

▨ Morning only

▧ Morning & evening

▦ Evening only

Proportion of Churches with morning and evening services

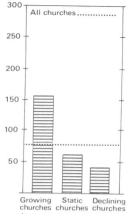

Average number of adults attending weekly services

	Percentage of churches which between 1980 & 1984:			Version of the Bible most used:		1984 Adults attending twice on Sunday	1984 Churches whose Services were held:			Mid-week meetings 1984:	
	Grew	Remained Static	Declined	Sunday	Mid-week Meetings		Morning only	Morn. & Evening	Evening only	Churches with	Average attendance
	%	%	%			%	%	%	%	%	
Church of Scotland	29	36	35	NEB	GNB	8	83	16	1	32	12
Conservative Presbyterian[3]	0	100	0	AV	AV	52	0	75	25	100	10
Scottish Episcopal	27	53	20	Various	AV	14	60	33	7	44	7
Baptist[3]	17	50	33	AV	AV	34	0	100	0	100	13
Independent	30	70	0	AV	AV	52	30	50	20	75	16
Other Denominations	19	67	14	AV	AV	34	52	34	14	76	15
All Protestant	26	46	28	AV	AV	21	69	26	5	45	12
Roman Catholic	7	57	36	JER	JER	0	57	36	7	29	13
All Churches	25	47	28	AV	AV	17	68	27	5	45	13

	1984 Sizes of Sunday Congregations[1]								Average Congregation per Church[2]
Number of adult attenders[2]	Under 10	10-25	26-50	51-100	101-150	151-200	201-300	Over 300	
	%	%	%	%	%	%	%	%	
All Protestant Churches	5	22	22	25	10	9	5	2	77
Growing Churches	0	7	7	21	19	23	14	9	154
Static Churches	7	25	20	31	11	5	1	0	59
Declining Churches	7	30	39	22	0	0	2	0	39
Roman Catholic Churches	0	14	0	29	14	7	7	29	163

This table is based on responses from 76% of all the churches in Tayside other than Dundee
Morning and evening services combined where both held excluding twicers

WESTERN ISLES AND SKYE & LOCHALSH

Total Adult Population:	31,350
Change of adult population in four years:	+2%
Total child population (under 15):	9,310
Change of child population in four years:	−1%
Total number of churches:	183
Percentage of churches responding:	58%
Total number of ministers:	96
Percentage of churches holding mid-week meetings:	67%
1984 adult Protestant church membership as percentage of total adult population:	59%
1984 Roman Catholic church membership as percentage of total adult population:	12%
1984 adult church attenders (Protestant and Roman Catholic) as percentage of total adult population:	54%
1984 adult church adherents as percentage of total adult population:	19%

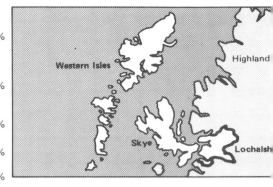

	Child Attenders			Adult Attenders			Membership			Average Sunday Congregation
	1980	1984	Change	1980	1984	Change	1980	1984	Change	1984
			%			%			%	Adults
Church of Scotland	1,930	**1,770**	−8	5,630	**5,060**	−10	3,430	**3,350**	−2	115
Conservative Presbyterian	2,600	**2,110**	−19	11,160	**9,870**	−12	16,720[4]	**14,290[4]**	−15	92
Scottish Episcopal	30	**30**	0	190	**180**	−5	370	**520**	+41	30
Baptist	0	**0**	-	0	**0**	-	0	**0**	-	-
Independent	30	**30**	0	90	**90**	0	100	**100**	0	44
Other Denominations	20	**20**	0	40	**40**	0	10	**10**	0	40
TOTAL Protestant	4,610	**3,960**	−14	17,110	**15,240**	−11	20,640	**18,280**	−11	95
Roman Catholic	350	**380**	+9	1,440	**1,560**	+8	3,820[3]	**3,720[3]**	−3	68
TOTAL All Churches	4,960	**4,340**	−12	18,550	**16,800**	−9	24,460	**22,000**	−10	92

	Church Attenders[2]			Civil Population		
Age Group	Male	Female	Total	Male	Female	Total
	%	%	%	%	%	%
Under 15	10	13	23	12	11	23
15-19	3	4	7	4	4	8
20-29	5	4	9	7	5	12
30-44	7	5	15	9	8	17
45-64	11	13	24	10	11	21
65 or over	8	14	22	8	11	19
All ages	44	56	100	50	50	100

[1] Morning and evening congregations combined where both held excluding twicers
[2] This table is based on responses from 43% of all the Protestant churches in the Western Isles and Skye & Lochalsh
[3] Total Catholic population including children
[4] Conservative Presbyterian adherents included with members

WESTERN ISLES AND SKYE & LOCHALSH

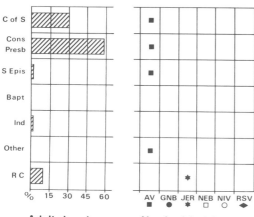

Adult churchgoers
by denominational
proportion

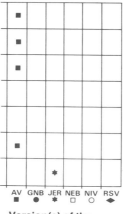

Version(s) of the
Bible used publicly
on Sunday

Proportion of
Churches with
morning and
evening services

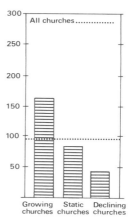

Average number of
adults attending
weekly services

	Percentage of churches which between 1980 & 1984:			Version of the Bible most used:		1984 Adults attending twice on Sunday	1984 Churches whose Services were held:			Mid-week meetings 1984:	
	Grew	Remained Static	Declined	Sunday	Mid-week Meetings		Morning only	Morn. & Evening	Evening only	Churches with	Average attendance
	%	%	%			%	%	%	%	%	
Church of Scotland	27	46	27	AV	AV	39	15	79	6	82	32
Conservative Presbyterian	16	60	24	AV	AV	48	7	68	25	62	22
Scottish Episcopal[3]	50	25	25	AV	AV/RSV	7	75	25	0	50	12
Baptist	–	–	–	–	–	–	–	–	–	–	–
Independent	*	*	*	*	*	*	0	100	0	*	*
Other Denominations	*	*	*	AV	AV	14	0	100	0	*	6
All Protestant	23	52	25	AV	AV	45	13	70	17	69	25
Roman Catholic[3]	40	60	0	JER	JER	2	67	33	0	43	10
All Churches	23	54	23	AV	AV	43	16	68	16	67	25

	1984 Sizes of Sunday Congregations[1]								Average Congregation per Church[2]
Number of adult attenders[2]	Under 10	10-25	26-50	51-100	101-150	151-200	201-300	Over 300	
	%	%	%	%	%	%	%	%	
All Protestant Churches	4	25	25	18	10	6	6	6	95
Growing Churches	5	5	10	10	28	19	10	14	161
Static Churches	2	31	25	20	6	4	6	6	82
Declining Churches	9	31	39	17	0	0	4	0	42
Roman Catholic Churches	*	*	*	*	*	*	*	*	68

This table is based on responses from 54% of all the churches in Western Isles and Skye & Lochalsh
Where held morning and evening services combined excluding twicers
Percentages unreliable because based on a particularly small number of churches
Too few churches to give a meaningful figure

103

SCOTTISH CENSUS 1984

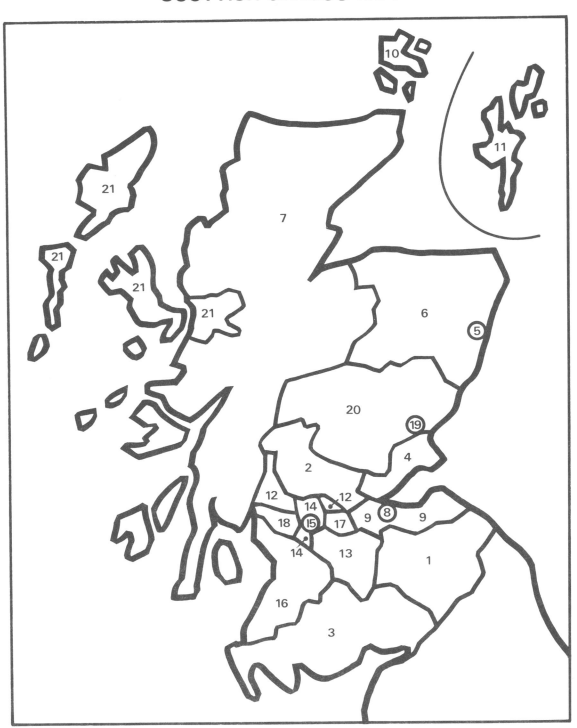

KEY TO AREAS USED IN MAP OPPOSITE

1 Borders
2 Central
3 Dumfries and Galloway
4 Fife
5 Grampian: Aberdeen
6 Grampian: Other
7 Highland excluding skye & Lochalsh but including Argyll & Bute
8 Lothian: Edinburgh
9 Lothian: Other
10 Orkney Islands
11 Shetland Islands
12 Strathclyde: Dumbarton, Clydebank and Cumbernauld & Kilsyth
13 Strathclyde: East Kilbride, Hamilton & Lanark
14 Strathclyde: Eastwood, Bearsden & Milngavie, and Strathkelvin
15 Strathclyde: Glasgow
16 Strathclyde: Kyle & Carrick, Cumnoch & Doun Valley, Kilmarnock & Loudoun, & Cunninghame
17 Strathclyde: Motherwell and Monklands
18 Strathclyde: Renfrew & Inverclyde
19 Tayside: Dundee
20 Tayside: Other
21 Western Isles and Skye & Lochalsh

ADDITIONAL DIAGRAMS FOR INDEPENDENT CHURCHES (SEE P.47)

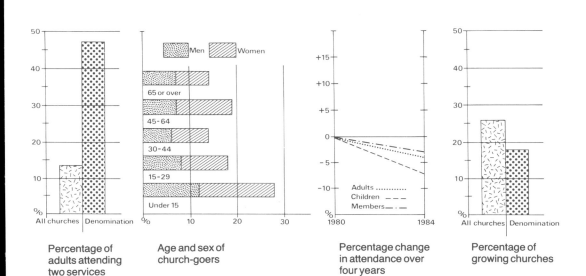

Percentage of adults attending two services

Age and sex of church-goers

Percentage change in attendance over four years

Percentage of growing churches

Also available

PROSPECTS FOR THE EIGHTIES

From a census of the Churches in 1979 undertaken by the Nationwide Initiative in Evangelism.

This historic survey of church-going in England, published in 1980, was the first occasion of joint co-operation on a statistical project by all the major Christian groups in England. It was also the first time that both membership and attendance had been so uniformly explored. The result is a rich body of data which remains relevant and which has been extensively used in other studies.

The overall picture is quite encouraging. In 1979 there were over 39,000 Christian churches in England; adult church attendance was 11% of the total population; the decline in attendance for the larger Protestant groups was slower than the decline in membership – hence less nominalism – and attendance was increasing for the smaller denominations.

Overall attendance in the Protestant churches was slightly on the increase.

Information is listed on a county by county basis, in each case showing changes in membership and attendance patterns, by denomination, and also showing the age/sex composition of those who attend church.

The volume includes a number of illuminating essays by Gavin Reid, Eddie Gibbs, Roger Forster and others.

Published by Bible Society and MARC Europe. Available from Bible Society and MARC Europe.

Vol. 1 – £3.00   Vol. 2 – £3.95

PROSPECTS FOR WALES

Edited by Byron Evans and Peter Brierley

From a census of Welsh churches undertaken by Bible Society and MARC Europe in 1982.

This survey was undertaken at the request of Wales for Christ, with the blessing of the Council of Churches for Wales. The results will encourage and challenge.

For each county in Wales a wealth of information is given, covering adult and child attendance, membership, congregation size, language, number of services and the percentage of growing churches. This detail is complemented by an extensive series of essays examining the state of the different denominations in Wales today.

Published jointly by Bible Society and MARC Europe. Available in English *and* Welsh.   £4.95

BEYOND THE CHURCHES

Facing a Task Unfinished

Edited by Peter Brierley

Beyond the Churches is a trail-blazer, a resource tool to stimulate evangelism. About 35 million adults in England and Wales do *not* go to church – how do we reach them? Before we can offer a solution we must clarify the problem.

With the support of the Evangelical Alliance MARC Europe has carried out a survey of unreached 'people groups' in England and Wales. More than 500 groups are listed, county by county – only a fraction of the total, but an indication of how the enormous task can be tackled.

Published by MARC Europe jointly with the Evangelical Alliance.   £4.95

UK CHRISTIAN HANDBOOK

Edited by Peter Brierley

Lists nearly 3,000 addresses of Christian organisations in the UK, with telephone numbers, key personnel, aims turnover etc. Fully illustrated, the *UK Christian Handbook* is an inavaluable reference tool for ministers, managers and administrators. '*A mine of information'* (Donald English).

Published jointly with the Evangelical Alliance and Bible Society.   £10.95 (paperback)   £15.95 (hardback)